How to
Explain a
Brain

How to Explain a Brain

An Educator's Handbook of Brain Terms and Cognitive Processes

Robert Sylwester

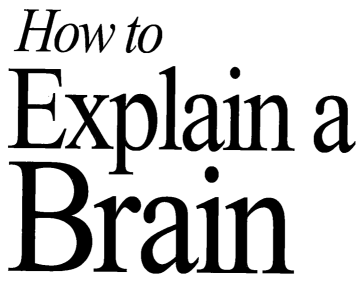 CORWIN PRESS
A Sage Publications Company
Thousand Oaks, California

KH

Illustrations by Peter Sylwester.

For information:

Corwin Press
A Sage Publications Company
2455 Teller Road
Thousand Oaks, California 91320
www.corwinpress.com

Sage Publications Ltd.
1 Oliver's Yard
55 City Road
London EC1Y 1SP
United Kingdom

Sage Publications India Pvt. Ltd.
B-42, Panchsheel Enclave
Post Box 4109
New Delhi 110 017 India

Printed in the United States of America

Library of Congress Cataloging-in-Publication Data

Sylwester, Robert.
How to explain a brain: An educator's handbook of brain terms and cognitive
processes / Robert Sylwester.
     p. cm.
Includes bibliographical references and index.
ISBN 1-4129-0638-5 (cloth)—ISBN 1-4129-0639-3 (pbk.)
    1. Neurosciences—Dictionaries. 2. Cognitive neuroscience—Dictionaries.
3. Brain—Dictionaries. I. Title.
RC334.S98 2005
612.8′03—dc22
                                    2004013831

04   05   06   07   10   9   8   7   6   5   4   3   2   1

Acquisitions Editor:	Faye Zucker
Editorial Assistant:	Stacy Wagner
Production Editor:	Melanie Birdsall
Copy Editor:	Elizabeth Budd
Typesetter:	C&M Digitals (P) Ltd.
Proofreader:	Cheryl Rivard
Indexer:	Michael Ferreira
Cover Designer:	Tracy E. Miller

11\21\06

Contents

List of Entries

Obsessive-Compulsive Disorder
Occipital Lobes
Olfactory Bulb. *See* Smell
Oligodendrocyte. *See* Glia
Operant Conditioning. *See* Conditioning
Oxytocin

Parallel Processing
Paranoia
Parasympathetic Nervous System. *See* Peripheral Nervous
    System
Parietal Lobes
Parkinson's Disease. *See* Cognitive and Motor Degeneration
Parvocellular. *See* Sight
Peptide. *See* Neurotransmitter
Perception
Peripheral Nervous System
PET (Positron Emission Tomography). *See* Brain
    Imaging Technology
Pheromone
Phoneme
Pia Mater. *See* Meninges
Pineal Gland
Pituitary Gland
Planum Temporale
Plasticity
Play and Games
Pons. *See* Hindbrain
Postsynaptic Neuron
Prefrontal Cortex. *See* Frontal Lobes
Presynaptic Neuron
Problem Solving
Procedural Memory. *See* Memory
Psychiatry. *See* Brain Sciences
Psychosis
Puberty and Adolescence
Pulvinar
Purkinje Cell. *See* Cerebellum
Pyramidal Cell. *See* Neuron

Preface

Recent dramatic advances in our understanding of the human brain and cognition ensure that the cognitive neurosciences will play an increasingly important role in educational policy and practice during the 21st century. Imaging technology can now directly observe and report the brain activity of subjects engaged in a wide variety of experimental cognitive tasks, and this has led to a better understanding of the neuronal substrate of learning, thought, and behavior. That knowledge is leading to the development of successful treatments for learning disabilities—and it will also lead to improvements in teaching and learning in normal classroom settings.

The biological sciences will also affect educational policy and practice in other important ways. Developments in genetics and neuroscience are already raising complex moral, ethical, political, cultural, financial, and religious issues, and we can expect a contentious increase in such issues. Citizens in a democratic society will thus need a functional understanding of the biology of genetics and cognition if they are to make wise decisions on issues such as cloning and stem cell research and on proposed educational procedures that emerge out of cognitive neuroscience research.

A third-grade student today will be a voter in 10 years. Think of all the developments in biology that have occurred during the past 10 years, and project what might occur before our third-grader votes. Much more biology (and specifically cognitive neuroscience concepts and processes) will thus need to be inserted into the K–12 curriculum.

The typical K–12 educator currently lacks the biological background to do this effectively because teaching has historically been much more oriented to the social and behavioral sciences than to biology. This made sense in an era in which biology didn't focus on teaching-learning processes. Although the social sciences similarly didn't focus on teaching and learning, their focus on group behavior was useful to teachers who work with students in a social setting. It thus isn't surprising that most preservice elementary teachers and many secondary teachers major in the social sciences.

Except for secondary school science teachers, few K–12 educators have the extensive academic preparation in chemistry, biology, and cognitive neuroscience that a 21st-century teacher will need. Furthermore, it will be difficult to insert more science coursework into an already packed teacher education program.

Conferences, staff development programs, and personal reading are currently helping to increase many teachers' cognitive neuroscience knowledge. It is perhaps only a bootstrapped beginning, but what are our options? This book assumes that in the foreseeable future, individual effort will be the principal venue for increasing the education profession's knowledge of the cognitive neurosciences. I sense that you agree with me because you probably wouldn't be reading this book if you didn't.

You will thus confront two challenges as you seek to increase your understanding of the cognitive neurosciences: First, to master the principal concepts and terms, and second, to teach the concepts and terms to your students and explain them to patrons.

ORIGIN OF THE BOOK

The book had its beginnings in the early 1960s. Whenever I ran into an unfamiliar brain or biology term or concept in my reading and work, I created one or more pages for the term's definition plus background and supplementary information that I had culled from dictionaries, glossaries, and texts and I then alphabetized the pages into a growing stack. These pages of written definitions changed over time as I continued to read, and as I tried to explain the concepts in non-technical terms to preservice and inservice educators. My initial audiences would typically look bewildered as I attempted to explain a technical concept, but after fine-tuning an explanation over subsequent presentations, I eventually would happily discover that folks were writing down my definition. I incorporated my successful explanations into presentation handouts, articles, books, and the monthly column I've written for the acclaimed Internet journal *Brain Connection* since the turn of the century (www.brainconnection. com). And so my very personal, loose, informal, cognitive neuroscience encyclopedia grew. This book is kind of like stapling the left margins of my considerably updated 40-plus-year pile of encyclopedic pages.

It was a stimulating experience to go through my own files and published work as well as recent reports on exciting developments, decide which terms and concepts to include in this book, and then update what I had written earlier to reflect current knowledge. It's amazing how the cognitive neurosciences have matured during my career—and it's similarly amazing to realize how much we have yet to learn about our brain and its cognitive processes.

How to Use the Book

This encyclopedic handbook is designed to help you when you confront unfamiliar brain concepts and terms in your reading and work. Articles and books on our brain often lack a glossary, and many of the definitions they do provide are technical—not expressed in functional terms that educators can understand and use with students. Furthermore, readers often need to refresh their memory of a definition during subsequent encounters with the word, and it's often difficult to locate the original definition. This reader-friendly companion book will thus be a useful nontechnical resource to enhance your understanding of brain terms and cognitive processes.

The book contains close to 300 entries and cross references, covering the range of concepts and terms that you will confront when reading about educationally significant developments in the cognitive neurosciences. Entries will typically comprise two parts: (1) an initial short functional definition of the concept or term and (2) an expanded commentary that will provide useful background and supplementary information for subsequent use in student instruction and patron discussions. Reproducible schematic models and illustrations focused on key brain functions will further enhance your understanding and use of the concepts and terms.

As indicated earlier, the terms included in the book represent my selection of the educationally significant concepts you're most apt to confront in your work. I've linked brain terms in the text to the relevant schematic illustrations at the front of the book. I've also included Internet addresses of the best related Web sites and a selected list of recent useful books for general readers. These resources should prove especially helpful to you if you want to track down an obscure term or the precise location of a brain structure that's difficult to depict in this book's schematic illustrations. For easy access to more than 1,500 detailed Internet illustrations of brain structures and systems, try using the BrainInfo database (http://braininfo.rprc.washington.edu/mainmenu.htmb) and the Whole Brain Atlas (www.med.harvard.edu/AANLIB/home.html).

Finally, my e-mail address is bobsyl@darkwing.uoregon.edu. If you don't understand something I've written or if you want information on a concept that isn't included in this book and can't easily locate it in a Web site, e-mail me and I'll respond quickly.

I've enjoyed my long journey toward understanding my brain and its cognitive processes—and I wish the same pleasure for you.

ACKNOWLEDGMENTS

Corwin Press extends its thanks to the following reviewers for their contributions to this book:

Robin Fogarty, Ph.D., President, Robin Fogarty & Associates, Chicago, IL

Kathie Nunley, Ed.D., Educational Consultant, Founder of www.brains.org, Amherst, NH

About the Author

 **Robert Sylwester** is an Emeritus Professor of Education at the University of Oregon who focuses on the educational implications of new developments in science and technology. He is the author of several books and many journal articles. His most recent book is *A Biological Brain in a Cultural Classroom: Enhancing Cognitive and Social Development Through Collaborative Classroom Management* (2003, 2nd ed., Corwin Press). The Education Press Association of America has given him two Distinguished Achievement Awards for his syntheses of cognitive science research, published in *Educational Leadership*. He has made more than 1,400 conference and inservice presentations on educationally significant developments in brain-stress theory and research. He writes a monthly column for the acclaimed Internet journal *Brain Connection* (www.brainconnection.com). He can be contacted at bobsyl@darkwing.uoregon.edu.

About the Illustrator

Peter Sylwester is a computer graphics designer who developed the illustrations for this book. His Web site is http://www.ptrdo.com, and his e-mail address is ptr@ptrdo.com.

Standard Hierarchy of Brain Areas

The major brain divisions identified below with their standard names are drawn from the BrainInfo database: http://braininfo.rprc.washington.edu/mainmenu.htmb.

The database provides information on 12,200 neuroanatomic terms and shows the hierarchical relationships among our brain's 550 primary brain structures; 1,500 illustrations enhance the usefulness of this fine resource.

HINDBRAIN
    Medulla Oblongata
    Metencephalon
        Cerebellum
        Pons

MIDBRAIN
    Cerebral Peduncle
    Tectum

FOREBRAIN
    Diencephalon
        Subthalamus
        Hypothalamus
        Thalamus
        Epithalamus
    Telencephalon
        Cerebral Cortex
        Cerebral White Matter

  Basal Ganglia
  Septum
 Fornix
 Olfactory Bulb

SOURCE: Braininfo. (2000). Neuroscience Division, Regional Primate Research Center, University of Washington. Retrieved from http://braininfo.rprc.washington.edu.

The Whole Brain Atlas is another excellent source of illustrations of brain structures and systems: www.med.harvard.edu/AANLIB/home.html.

Schematic Illustrations

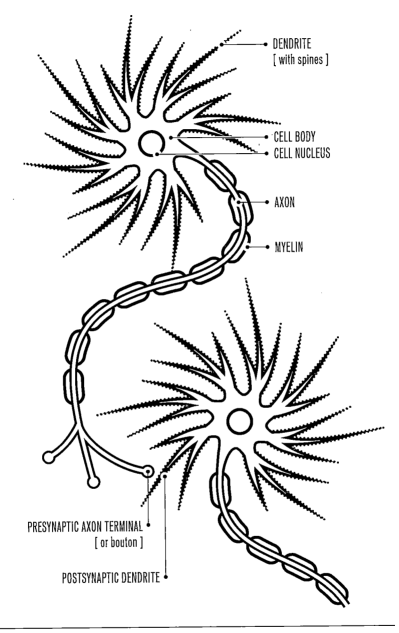

Figure 1   Schematic Model of Two Related Neurons

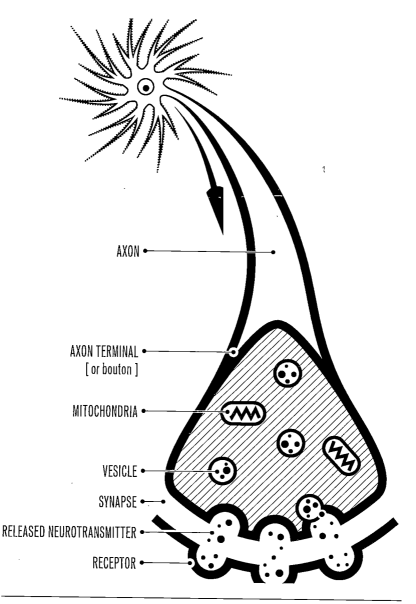

AXON

AXON TERMINAL
[or bouton]

MITOCHONDRIA

VESICLE

SYNAPSE

RELEASED NEUROTRANSMITTER

RECEPTOR

Figure 2   Schematic of Synaptic Transmission

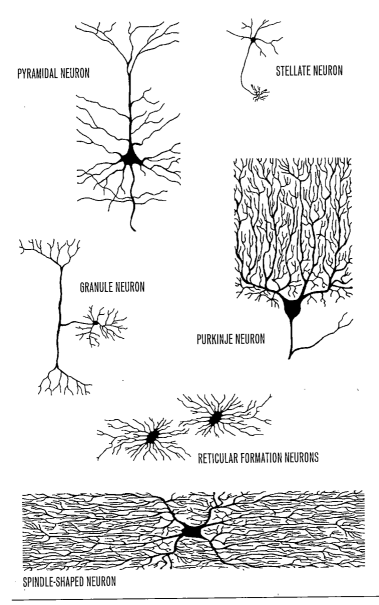

Figure 3   Examples of Neuron Variation

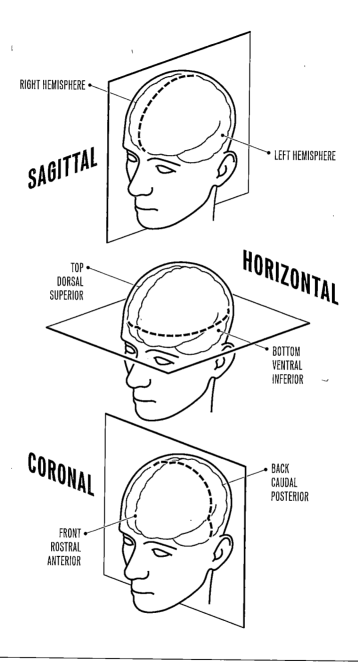

Figure 4   Sectional Planes

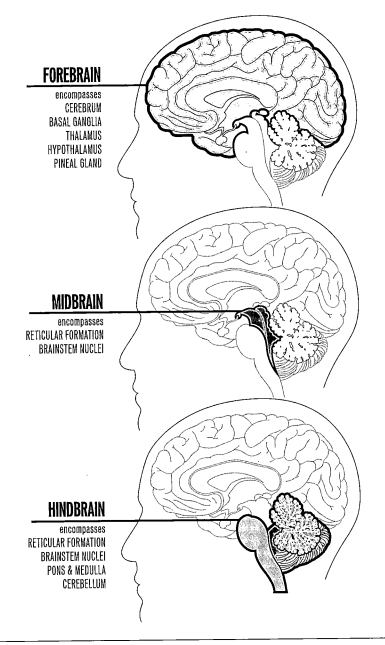

FOREBRAIN
encompasses
CEREBRUM
BASAL GANGLIA
THALAMUS
HYPOTHALAMUS
PINEAL GLAND

MIDBRAIN
encompasses
RETICULAR FORMATION
BRAINSTEM NUCLEI

HINDBRAIN
encompasses
RETICULAR FORMATION
BRAINSTEM NUCLEI
PONS & MEDULLA
CEREBELLUM

Figure 5   Hindbrain, Midbrain, and Forebrain

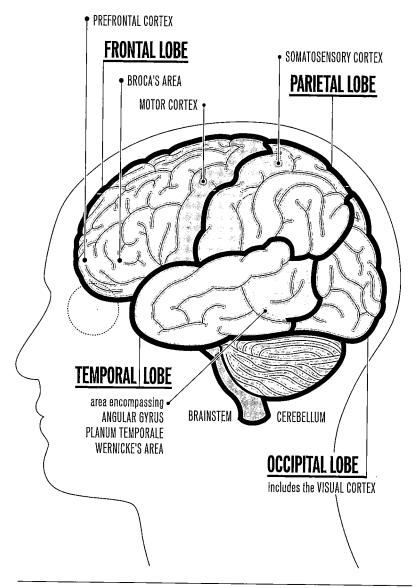

PREFRONTAL CORTEX

FRONTAL LOBE

SOMATOSENSORY CORTEX

BROCA'S AREA

PARIETAL LOBE

MOTOR CORTEX

TEMPORAL LOBE

area encompassing
ANGULAR GYRUS   BRAINSTEM   CEREBELLUM
PLANUM TEMPORALE
WERNICKE'S AREA

OCCIPITAL LOBE

includes the VISUAL CORTEX

Figure 6   Major Cerebral Cortex Regions

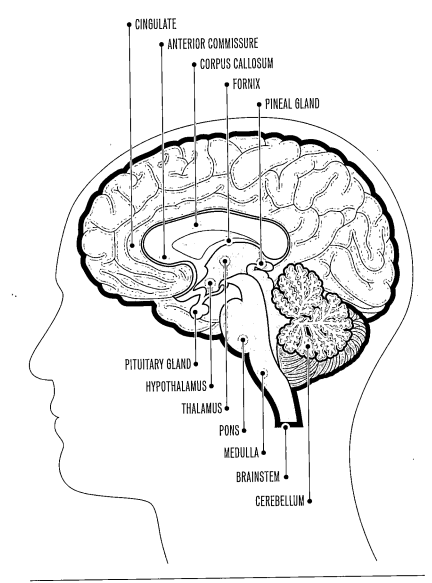

Figure 7   Selected Interior Brain Systems: Side View

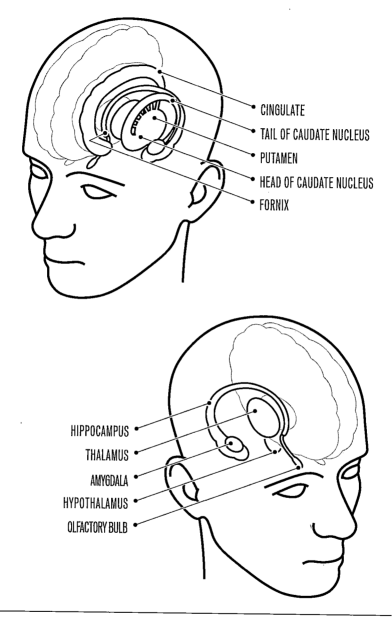

- CINGULATE
- TAIL OF CAUDATE NUCLEUS
- PUTAMEN
- HEAD OF CAUDATE NUCLEUS
- FORNIX

- HIPPOCAMPUS
- THALAMUS
- AMYGDALA
- HYPOTHALAMUS
- OLFACTORY BULB

Figure 8   Selected Interior Brain Systems: Front Views

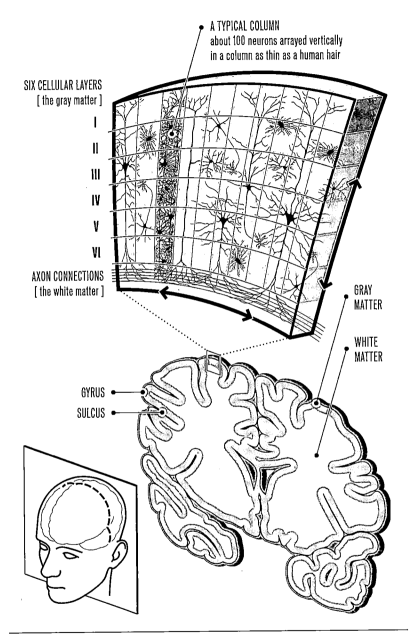

Figure 9   Schematic of Coronal Section

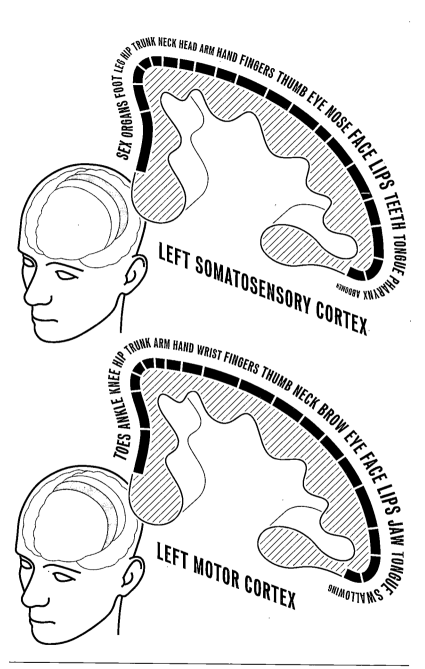

Figure 10   Somatosensory and Motor Cortex Areas

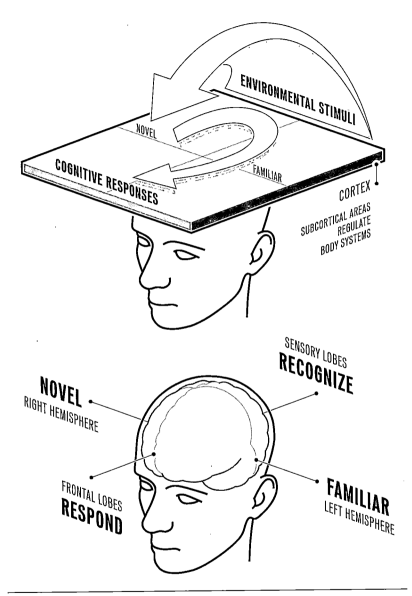

Figure 11   Stylized View of Brain Functions

Alphabetized Entries

A

Acetylcholine (A-set-tul-KO-leen)

The first neurotransmitter discovered (1921).

Acetylcholine is distributed throughout our brain and especially in centers controlling conscious movement (such as the basal ganglia and motor cortex). It regulates all voluntary muscles and many involuntary muscles, and it's the primary neurotransmitter for the parasympathetic nervous system (rest and recuperation). It's estimated that as many as 10% of our brain's synapses use acetylcholine, and its action is generally excitatory. It's also active in learning and memory circuits. People with Alzheimer's disease suffer from a depletion of functional acetylcholine neurons in the hippocampus.

See also Basal Ganglia, Hippocampus, Motor Cortex, Neuron, Neurotransmitter, Peripheral Nervous System

Action Potential. *See* Neuron

Adolescence. *See* Puberty and Adolescence

Adrenaline

A molecule that can function both as a hormone (synthesized in the adrenal glands) and as a neurotransmitter (called epinephrine). It

15

helps to activate body-brain systems, especially during stress responses.

See also Hormones, Neurotransmitter

Agnosia (ag-NO-zhuh)

A condition in which people with a functioning sensory system are unable to recognize objects, people, places, or events that should be familiar. Agnosia means "not knowing."

Agnosia typically occurs because of damage to specific brain regions that interpret sensory information. Other interpretive regions may be functional. For example, someone with prosopagnosia can't recognize a friend's face but can recognize her voice; someone with color agnosia can't recognize different colors despite functioning visual and language systems; and someone with gustatory agnosia can't recognize and discriminate among tastes.

See also Aphasia

Agraphia. *See* Aphasia

Alpha Waves. *See* Brain Waves

Alzheimer's Disease. *See* Cognitive and Motor Degeneration

Amino Acid (a-MEE-no)

The chemical building blocks of proteins and of neurotransmitters.

Four types of molecules provide the construction base of all organisms: amino acids, fatty acids, nucleotides, and sugars. Amino acids and peptides (small combinations of amino acids) can function as neurotransmitters, and longer amino acid chains and proteins can function as the receptors on neurons to which neurotransmitters attach and pass information from the presynaptic to the postsynaptic neuron.

See also Neuron, Neurotransmitter

Amnesia (am-NEE-zhuh)

A breakdown of part or all of the cognitive processes that store and recall memories.

Amnesia can result from trauma, disease, tumor, stroke, or dementia occurring in the brain regions that process memory and from encephalitis or chronic alcoholism (Korsakoff's syndrome). Amnesia most often occurs in our long-term declarative (factual and autobiographical) memory systems. Although many specific kinds of memory loss have been clinically identified, retrograde and anterograde amnesia are perhaps the most common (and some people suffer from both).

Retrograde amnesia is the inability to recall any declarative information that was stored prior to the damage (which typically occurred in the temporal lobe areas that are central to the processing of declarative memories).

Anterograde amnesia is the inability to store and recall declarative information that emerges after damage to declarative memory processing systems, although these amnesiacs can recall information from periods prior to the damage. Perhaps the best-known case of anterograde amnesia is a man commonly called HM who had most of his hippocampus and amygdala surgically removed at age 27 (1953) in an attempt to stop his epileptic seizures. It helped his epilepsy but left him with profound anterograde amnesia. Since then, HM has been unable to store or recall any new declarative information, although he can recall memories from before the surgery, and he can develop new procedural (skill) memories. He basically lives within the world of short-term memory (a few minutes at most). HM became the most-studied amnesiac in medical history, and much of what scientists initially learned about declarative memory and amnesia resulted from these studies.

You could functionally explain amnesia as follows: Think of a computerized warehouse in which materials are stored before being retrieved and sent to customers. Suppose that the computer and database that contain the location of the stored materials becomes dysfunctional. That would be a situation somewhat similar to retrograde amnesia. Suppose again that new shipments of materials arrived to be stored within the warehouse, but the dysfunctional computer and database can't specify where the new materials should be stored. That would be a situation somewhat similar to anterograde amnesia. See Figures 6 and 8.

See also Amnesia, Hippocampus, Memory

Amygdala (ah-MIG-da-lah)

A paired complex of structures the shape and size of an almond that recognize innate biological fears and activate relevant primal automatic responses. It is often called the "Fear Button."

The amygdala is located in the lower frontal areas of the two temporal lobes. Place a finger on either temple, and an amygdala will be about 1.5 inches into your brain.

If incoming sensory information that passes through the amygdala portends imminent danger (such as a sudden movement or loud sound), the amygdala will rapidly signal the nearby hypothalamus to initiate an appropriate response (fight, flight, freeze). Fearful information is simultaneously sent into the cingulate area of the cortex for conscious thought about alternate responses if the danger isn't imminent. The amygdala also adds positive and negative emotional content to the memory of an experience for use in subsequent similar situations, thus playing an important role in the consolidation of long-term memories that occurs in various brain areas. See Figure 8.

See also Amnesia, Cingulate Gyrus, Hypothalamus, Stress

Angiotensin II (an-jee-o-TEN-sin 2)

A peptide that triggers drinking behaviors when body fluid levels are low.

See also Neuron, Neurotransmitter

Angular Gyrus (AN-gyu-lar JI-rus)

A (typically) left-hemisphere region located posterior to Wernicke's area, at the juncture of the occipital, parietal, and temporal lobes. It connects the initial visual word recognition process to other elements of language comprehension and production that are principally processed in forward regions of our brain. See Figure 6.

   See also Cerebral Cortex, Wernicke's Area

Anterior Cingulate Gyrus. *See* Cingulate Gyrus

Anterior Commissure (KOM-i-sure)

   A commissure is a bundle of myelinated axons that link and exchange information between the two cerebral hemispheres. The anterior commissure exchanges emotional information between the unconscious subcortical areas of the two hemispheres. It's located below and toward the front of the corpus callosum, a much larger commissure that exchanges conscious thought between the hemispheres. Some evidence exists that both commissures are typically larger in females than in males. See Figure 7.

   See also Cerebral Hemispheres, Corpus Callosum, Neuron

Anterograde Amnesia. *See* Amnesia

Anxiety

   An unpleasant emotional state that's focused on potentially negative events. It exists along a continuum from mild concern to intense fear.

   Emotional arousal occurs in response to a looming danger or opportunity. Anxiety adds a feeling of apprehension to emotional arousal—a feeling that a real or imagined challenge will result in a negative outcome because we lack the resources to respond successfully. It's normal for feelings of anxiety to emerge periodically during the course of the day as we try to meet a variety of commitments, but anxiety becomes dysfunctional when dread and doom dominate our thoughts and activities.

   Symptoms of a dysfunctional anxiety include irregularities in circulation, respiration, and appetite and digestion; headaches;

generalized aches and pains; fatigue; and an inability to relax. Phobias, panic disorder, and obsessive-compulsive disorder are some of the specific manifestations of dysfunctional anxiety. Such anxiety disorders emerge when a response that is normally appropriate and useful (such as fear of falling) becomes excessive and limiting (such as in refusing to use elevators or airplanes).

See also Stress

Aphasia (ah-FAY-zhuh)

A general term for an impaired ability or a complete loss of ability to understand or express some element of language.

Aphasia typically occurs following stroke or traumatic damage to some part of our brain's language-processing areas, or because of delayed brain development. Global aphasia is a complete inability to process language, but the lost function in the many other types of aphasia is limited and quite specific. Language is a complex activity that requires the collaboration of many separate brain areas. In nonglobal aphasia, one or more language-processing areas become dysfunctional, but others do not. For example, someone with anomia can't name specific people, objects, or places (or a combination of these), although they recognize them when others identify them; someone with tactile aphasia can't name touched unseen objects but can name them if viewed; and someone with syntactic aphasia has trouble arranging words in their proper grammatical sequence. The best-known forms of aphasia are Wernicke's and Broca's aphasia. In Wernicke's aphasia, language comprehension is impaired but speech production is not (although speech tends to be error-laden). In Broca's aphasia, language comprehension is good, but speech is limited and labored at best.

Dyslexia is typically a developmental reading disability in an otherwise intelligent child or adult who is motivated to read and who has had adequate schooling. Dyslexia is not a generalized language defect, but a specific localized functional deficiency in the brain areas that process the sounds of language (phonemes). This results in difficulty in fluent word recognition, decoding, and spelling, which may lead to problems with reading comprehension and vocabulary development. Recent advances suggest that although it isn't an easily cured condition, early diagnosis and intense intervention can materially improve the reading capabilities of people with dyslexia.

Agraphia is the loss of writing ability, even though arm and hand movements are unimpaired. As with aphasia, an agraphic impairment can be quite specific. Someone with apraxic agraphia can orally spell words but can't easily write them; someone with spatial agraphia can't arrange text properly on a page. See Figure 6.

See also Agnosia, Broca's Area, Language, Wernicke's Area

Arachnoid Mater (a-RACK-noid MAH-ter).
See Meninges

Arcuate Fasciculus (ARK-u-ate fah-SICK-u-lus)

A (typically) left-hemisphere axon pathway that processes language. It originates in neurons in Wernicke's area in the temporal lobe, passes through the angular gyrus, and connects with Broca's area neurons in the frontal lobe. It thus moves language from the original thought impetus to the frontal lobe language production areas.

Think of it as being analogous to a transportation route that takes raw materials to a production site. See Figure 6.

See also Angular Gyrus, Broca's Area, Wernicke's Area

Arts

A celebration of conscious human skill and production that elevate ordinary behaviors or objects into something aesthetically extraordinary and transcendent. George Bernard Shaw suggested that we use a mirror to see our face and the arts to see our soul.

Artifacts from early human societies suggest that the arts were always cognitively important. If the arts hadn't been important, people wouldn't have expended the considerable time and energy it took to decorate clothing and tools and to make nonfunctional artistic objects (such as necklaces), given the primitive tools and materials available to them.

The arts have endured, and so we've also learned much about later cultures via their art. Anouilh, Bach, Cezanne, Da Vinci, and the rest of the arts alphabet live on in today's theaters, concert halls, and museums.

So why would communities who laud their architecture, museums, musical organizations, and theaters reduce or even eliminate their school arts programs that a quarter of a century ago were staffed by trained professionals? Do folks who enjoy choir music in church think that singing in choral parts is innate? Do small communities struggling for identity realize that their school arts program is just about the only live culture in the area?

What occurred was the emergence of a politically powerful but biologically naïve belief that it is necessary and possible to create an efficient, inexpensive, one-size-fits-all assessment program that precisely measures all the learned behaviors of an imprecise brain.

Some learned behavior (such as language and math skills and facts) can be precisely measured. The response is either true or false. But most human behavior involves making choices among legitimate alternatives, such as what TV shows to watch, what to order in a restaurant, what charities to support, and which candidate to vote for. These decisions generally don't emerge out of factual *true/false,* but out of personal beliefs about *right/wrong, good/bad, fair/unfair, beautiful/ ugly, interesting/boring,* and so on, that are often unrelated to factual information about the issue. The failures we experience in life generally occur because of poor personal, social, and vocational choices and not because of spelling or multiplication table deficiencies.

When politicians began to demand that educators create precise assessment programs, the arts were obviously in trouble. As suggested earlier, the arts are about personal choices that lead to unique creations that demonstrate style and grace, and not about programmed responses that lead to reproducible measurable correctness. Unfortunately, the assessment and standards movement gained momentum because of its appeal to folks who seek simple solutions to complex problems—and it now pretty much drives the curriculum.

Art programs are expensive and labor-intensive, and so they are also vulnerable on those accounts in a tight economy. Arts educators thus tried to accommodate the assessment movement by developing statements that justify their existence and by creating standards that could be assessed.

But why should the arts have to justify themselves? They have been integral to human life a lot longer than algebra and spelling, which evidently weren't required to justify their curricular existence. Yet is it possible to understand algebra without understanding symbolics and metaphor, central constructs of the arts?

One could further argue that if it's important for children to learn the sequence of letters that spell a word, it should be equally important to learn the sequence of tones that create a melody. Why would schools seek to develop only one of the brain mechanisms that have evolved to process such communication sequences? To justify music in school by suggesting that playing music calms down students in a classroom or on the school bus or that music somehow mysteriously improves math scores is to seriously miss the point about what the arts and arts education are all about.

Similarly, precise assessment of the arts is a hopeless enterprise, because the arts can't be narrowly defined, easily measured, and precisely reproduced. You can't box something that allows the human spirit to soar.

The poet e. e. cummings stated it beautifully: "Nothing measurable can be alive; nothing which is not alive can be art; nothing which cannot be art is true: and everything untrue doesn't matter a very good God damn . . ."[1]

Arts performance and products obviously can be and are evaluated. Critics do it all the time. Their criticism is subjective, however, and two critics may differ considerably on their assessment of the same artistic performance or product. The value of such critical assessment is thus dependent on the experience and credibility of the critic, and not solely on some external objective *true/false* measure, such as, "The concert pianist played 93.6% of the notes correctly."

The loss of teachers with professional training in the arts may well be the most serious in the diminution of arts education programs. It's foolish to demand credible assessment in the arts and then to eliminate the educators who were trained to do it.

The National Endowment for the Arts and the U.S. Department of Education funded an extensive study that analyzed the considerable arts education research literature in an attempt to resolve issues that relate to the assessment and standards movement and arts education. What emerged, *Critical Links: Learning in the Arts and Student Academic and Social Development* (Deasy, 2002), is an excellent, carefully selected compendium of 62 studies that the task force considered best able to help resolve the issue of the role of the arts in contemporary K–12 education.

Critical Links examined research studies and position papers in dance, drama, music, visual arts, and also studies that explored multi-arts issues. Many of the studies were meta-analyses of a large number of related studies. Educators interested in arts education or assessment and curricular standards should certainly read this thoughtful and thought-provoking analysis.

In essence, the project discovered that it is currently difficult, if not impossible, to identify substantive cognitive changes that occur quickly as a result of exposure to the arts. It takes at least 20 years for our brain to reach maturity, and arts abilities and values (like many other value-laden elements of life) emerge gradually.

Transfer in learning from one cognitive domain to another isn't a one-way process (such as the belief that the arts must improve reading scores to be of value). Rather, transfer is a reciprocal process in which all curricular areas in a good school provide support for the mastery of other areas.

The arts aren't about mastering specific measurable units of information, but about integrating information and values—and because integration can occur in a wide variety of ways and take many forms, simple assessment technologies that seek precise measurements are inappropriate for the central elements of a quality arts education program.

The 62 studies identified a number of important specific areas of cognitive maturation that a high-quality arts education program supports. Although this is useful information for educators beset by political pressures, the arts are really an exploratory enterprise that allows our brain to reconstruct the ordinary elements of our life and world into something extraordinary—*a celebration of the ordinary.* For those who purport to be human, what's more important in life and school than that?

NOTE: 1. From E. E. Cummings, *A Miscellany Revised,* edited by George Firmage. New York: October House, 1965. 314–15.

See also Music

Reference

Deasy, R. (Ed.). (2002). *Critical links: Learning in the arts and student academic and social development.* Washington, DC: Council of Chief State School Officers (One Massachusetts Ave., NW, Suite 700, Washington, DC 20001-1431; www.aep-arts.org).

Aspartate (AS-par-tate)

An amino acid that can act as an excitatory neurotransmitter.

See also Neuron, Neurotransmitter

Asperger's Syndrome. *See* Autism

Astrocyte. *See* Glia

Attention

Attention is our brain's focusing system that is activated by emotional arousal.

Emotional arousal indicates the presence of a looming challenge. Attention is a complex cognitive system that selects and temporarily focuses on key emotionally important elements in an often-confusing environment and maintains goal-directed behavior in highly distractible situations. It thus psychologically separates an emotionally significant foreground from the less significant background. Think of the frame on a picture, the zoom lens on a camera, traffic arrows, and the stage in an auditorium as technologies that help to direct our attention—separating foreground from background.

Our attentional system is composed of a number of distinct neural networks, each of which actively carries out specific attentional functions.

The orienting system disengages us from what we were attending to and focuses us on the new challenge. We generally shift our attention to objects and events that contrast sharply with our current focus and ignore (or merely monitor) steady states, subtle differences, and gradual changes that don't carry a sense of immediacy. For example, we tend to ignore a constant temperature but attend to a sudden change.

Our environment, however, is replete with serious subtle and gradual dangers (such as pollution). These are emotionally significant, but we tend to focus on them only when a high-contrast catastrophe (such as a toxic spill) occurs. The *news* is about the unusual, not the normal, and so it reports a single freeway pileup of 10 cars, but not the 100 individual fender-benders that occur in the same general area that day. Graphs and time-lapse photography are technological aids we've developed to observe changes that occur too gradually to activate our biological emotion and attention systems.

The executive attention system draws heavily on memory to recognize the identity of the new challenge (foreground), determine its significance, and separate it from the background information (which it then merely monitors or ignores). This is typically an efficient unconscious process that draws on established responses, but we do confront situations in which it is not obvious what we should focus on within a confusing setting. In such situations, our executive attention system must consciously make the decision—such as to respond to a novel situation that will require planning and decision making, to alter a habitual response, or to correct an error.

Our working brain (or working memory) is an important part of this system. It is a fragile, limited-capacity buffer that allows us to attend to and briefly hold a few units of information while we use it (e.g., dial the phone number) or determine its importance (e.g., the name of a stranger who joins a party conversation). It's about things that are important right now, but not so important that we want to remember them for the rest of our life. The limited capacity of our working brain is useful, because it forces us to combine related bits of information into larger units by identifying similarities, differences, and patterns that can simplify and consolidate an otherwise large and confusing sensory field. Vocabulary categories emerged out of this cognitive ability.

The *vigilance system* has the reverse task of the orienting system. Vigilance maintains a sustained focus on something while ignoring small, random, potentially distracting environmental changes. The vigilance system thus helps us to ignore minor, but not major, distractions. A major distraction may lead to an emotional arousal that activates our orienting system, and we're off to a new focus of attention. We typically can simultaneously attend to several noncompeting events (such as to look at a person while conversing and putting on a coat), but not to competing events (such as to carry on two conversations simultaneously, one in person and one on the telephone).

As remarkable as our vigilance system is, it isn't good at sustaining attention on tasks that are oriented to precise details and contain only subtle environmental shifts. Many educational activities unfortunately require students to maintain vigilant attention in such situations (such as while solving a page of many similar math problems). Vigilance is an important component in most games children play (from tag to videogames), so they seem to have an almost innate sense that they need to develop the system. Many accidents involve attentional lapses.

Our three-part attention system thus moves us from arousal to focus. It's a sort of zoom lens that can zoom in to identify and carefully examine details (foreground) or zoom out to scan the context (background).

See also Emotion and Feelings, Memory

Attention-Deficit Disorder (ADD)

A class of behavioral disorders characterized by persistent inattention, impulsiveness, and often hyperactivity.

ADD is generally considered a childhood disorder that affects up to 10% of the population, and three times as many boys as girls, but it can persist into adult life. Although educators have been especially concerned about ADHD (attention-deficit/hyperactivity disorder) because of its negative impact on classroom life, it is important to realize that malfunctions in one or more of the subsystems that regulate attention can lead to various mental illnesses and learning handicaps (such as anxiety, autism, bipolar disorder, dyslexia, hyperactivity, mental retardation, obsessive-compulsive disorder, and schizophrenia). Medications and behavioral interventions exist to help those whose deficits in one or more elements of the attentional system are related to chemical imbalances, developmentally weak neuronal pathways, or learned inappropriate behavior patterns.

See also Attention

Autism (AW-tizm)

An ill-understood condition characterized principally by extreme difficulty in emotional communication and social interaction, a preference for details and repetitive routine, and often a specific savant capability (such as the ability to multiply large numbers mentally) that extends well beyond the normal range. It appears during early childhood in 1 in 500 children, 80% of whom are male.

We are normally able to understand the behavior and intentions of people and also the principles that govern objects and systems. Females typically have a slight advantage in understanding people, compared with their male counterparts' advantage in understanding objects and systems. Autistic children have an exceptional ability to understand objects and systems at the expense of being able to understand people, and this may help to explain why more males are autistic.

Autism has a genetic component that manifests itself in brain organization and development. For example, the cerebellum is smaller, and brain systems and molecules associated with social behavior are often subnormal. Early childhood brain development is more rapid than normal, and this may lead to a sense of being overwhelmed by sensory information—and to a desire to withdraw.

A milder form of the condition, called Asperger's syndrome, is characterized by obsessive interests and an autistic lack of social skills, but also by a normal-to-high IQ and normally developing speech skills.

Although autism currently has no cure, programs of vigorous early intervention can help many autistic children move toward a more normal life. See Figures 5–7.

See also Cerebellum

Autonomic Nervous System. *See* Peripheral Nervous System

Axon. *See* Neuron

B

Basal Ganglia

A cluster of subcortical structures that work with several other brain systems (such as the motor cortex and cerebellum) to determine, plan, and regulate the initiation, coordination, and termination of voluntary movements.

Basal ganglia structures that carry out these processes include the globus pallidus and the striatum (an encompassing term for the caudate nucleus and putamen). In movement regulation, basal ganglia output is principally inhibitory, and cerebellar output is principally excitatory. The amygdala and substantia nigra are functionally connected to the basal ganglia.

Parkinson's disease and Huntington's disease are related to basal ganglia malfunctions and are characterized by a loss of movement control.

Recently the caudate nucleus has also emerged as an important structure in our brain's pleasure and reward circuitry, and so it's active during expressions of romantic love. See Figures 7 and 8.

See also Amygdala, Cerebellum, Cognitive and Motor Degeneration, Love, Substantia Nigra

Basket Cell. *See* Cerebellum

Belief and Knowledge

A *belief* is the acceptance of something as true, even though no conclusive evidence exists to validate it or any other competing belief on the issue. Something becomes *knowledge* when considerable generally accepted evidence exists to validate it but no other position on the issue.

Knowledge is thus about factual information—true/false. Belief is about preferences and choices—right/wrong, fair/unfair, moral/immoral, appropriate/inappropriate, beautiful/ugly. A person would *know* that the Bible is a widely used religious document and that the Republican and Democratic Parties dominate U.S. politics. A person would *believe* (or not believe) that the Bible is correct in every statement it makes or that one's favored political party is superior to the other.

Beta Waves. *See* Brain Waves

Binding

The means through which a variety of related interconnected neural networks coordinate their activity to produce a unified mental concept.

Imagine a red ball rolling across a table. Our brain contains separate areas that process color, shape, movement, and quantity, so the *binding problem* refers to how these brain areas coordinate their activities into a unified perception—for example, that the color *red* is inserted into that specific *round, moving* shape and not into some other object in our visual field. The current view of binding is that the neural networks that represent the various sensory (or imagined) elements of an attended-to entity somehow synchronize their firing rates at 40 hertz (40 neuronal firings per second).

Imagine a choir singing a song. If they all sing the same lyrics at the same tempo, we hear it as a synchronized song. If not, it's just incomprehensible noise. The synchronized singing thus becomes the attended-to foreground, and any other sounds in the room become meaningless ignored background noise. Our attentive brain similarly uses a synchronized neuronal firing rate to bind specific related elements into a unified entity that it can thus separate from the other elements of a complex external sensory (or internal imagined) environment.

Blood-Brain Barrier

A protective layer surrounding our brain's blood vessels (and especially capillaries) that allows useful materials to pass from the circulatory system into brain tissue but prevents most potentially dangerous materials from doing so. Astrocyte glial cells are a key element of the blood-brain barrier.

Our brain must tightly control its chemical balance, because a chemical imbalance can lead to mental illness. The blood-brain barrier is not a perfect system; drugs such as nicotine, alcohol, and heroin can pass through the barrier into brain tissue, but some potentially useful drugs can't. For example, dopamine is an important brain neurotransmitter, but people whose dopamine deficiency results in Parkinson's disease can't be treated with dopamine injections into their bloodstream because dopamine can't pass through the blood-brain barrier. However, a medication called L-Dopa, which includes the ingredients that make up dopamine, can pass through the blood-brain barrier, and so its entry into the brain provides the ingredients necessary for dopamine synthesis.

Our brain's blood-brain barrier and protective skull are thus key protective elements for our important but very vulnerable brain.

See also Dopamine, Drugs, Glia

Bouton. *See* Neuron

Brain

The major organ of the nervous system, which consists of the central nervous system (the brain and spinal cord) and the peripheral nervous system (the sensorimotor extensions into all other body areas). The nervous system is one of our body's four information-processing systems, the other three being the immune, endocrine gland, and circulatory systems.

The adult human brain is the best-organized, most functional three pounds of matter in the known universe. It's responsible for Beethoven's Ninth Symphony, computers, burglary, the Sistine Chapel, automobiles, the Second World War, *Hamlet,* apple pie, and a whole lot more.

The cellular mass of our brain is evenly divided between an estimated 100 billion highly interconnected neurons and about a trillion much smaller glial support cells. At the functional systems level, our brain is composed of (a) the relatively small brainstem region at the top of the spinal cord that unconsciously regulates such internal survival functions as circulation and respiration and synthesizes many of the neurotransmitters that regulate brain activity; (b) the much larger, two-hemisphere cerebrum that consciously recognizes and responds to external challenges and internal imagination; and (c) the cerebellum that plays a number of important supportive and coordinating roles in thought and action.

Our brain, with a consistency similar to refrigerated butter, is very vulnerable to damage, and so it's encased in a protective skull about the size of a coconut. The adult human brain weighs about 2% of our body weight, but it uses 20% of our body's energy, principally in the form of glucose. The arterial blood that leaves the heart goes to the brain first, so the brain takes whatever it needs to survive.

Our brain's overall task is to recognize and respond to novel and familiar dangers and opportunities that occur in our space-time world. This can become problematic because, for example, a danger in one situation can become an opportunity in another. We must similarly continually determine the point at which true becomes false, right becomes wrong, moral becomes immoral, fair becomes unfair, beautiful becomes ugly, and so on. Much brain space and energy are thus devoted to making and then acting on such distinctions. See Figures 5, 6, and 11.

See also Brainstem, Central Nervous System, Cerebellum, Cerebral Cortex, Cerebrum, Circulatory System, Endocrine Glands, Immune System, Movement, Neuron, Peripheral Nervous System

Brain Imaging Technology

Recently developed computerized machines that measure and display the variations in chemical composition, blood-flow patterns, and electromagnetic fields that occur in normal and abnormal brains.

Our skull protects our brain, but it also serves as a barrier to the direct observation of cognitive activity and to our brain's organization and development. Scientists who studied brain properties and functions 20-plus years ago were thus forced to experiment on animal brains, to study autopsied brains of people who had various cognitive or motor impairments, and to compare the behavior of people who had normal and abnormal brains. It was a difficult and principally inferential process.

Recent advances in computerized imaging technology have made it possible to *technologically* pass through the skull and brain tissue and to observe, amplify, record, rapidly analyze, and graphically display the brain substances and signals that reflect activity in very specific brain regions. This technology has revolutionized brain and mind research, and the diagnosis and treatment of many brain-related diseases and malfunctions.

The first imaging technologies, the X-ray and EEG (electroencephalogram), were primitive by today's standards, but both have been considerably improved—and provided the conceptual base of the other amazing imaging technologies that have recently emerged.

Computerized brain imaging technologies now measure and display the variations in chemical composition, blood-flow patterns, and electromagnetic fields that occur in normal and abnormal brains. Each of the several current forms of brain imaging technology has strengths and weaknesses, and new developments are continually making the technology faster, more powerful, less invasive, and less expensive. Imaging technology was initially used primarily in medical diagnosis, but it is increasingly being used in pure neuroscience and psychological research.

Educational researchers are just beginning to use imaging technologies, but this use will dramatically increase in the coming years. It will revolutionize educational research and many elements of educational policy and practice.

The various computerized imaging technologies differ, but the following analogy demonstrates how someone can examine internal differences in something (a brain) that has a protective cover (a skull): Imagine that you're looking for similarities, differences, and imperfections in successive slices of a thinly sliced apple or potato. A brain imaging machine is basically a camera that can rapidly and successively change its focus as it photographs and digitally stores successive thin *slices* of a brain to create a comprehensive three-dimensional image of selected properties of the entire brain.

The graphic displays in imaging technology typically use the color spectrum gradations to represent the activity levels of the various brain areas in a scan (the red end of the spectrum representing a high level of activity in a brain area, the purple end representing low activity, and the other colors representing intermediate levels). Topographical maps similarly use different colors to represent elevations (mountains, valleys, etc.). A scan of a slice of brain thus graphically indicates which brain areas were active and inactive during the time interval of the scan.

Functional magnetic resonance imaging (commonly written fMRI) measures brain blood-flow patterns and metabolic changes. Although almost a dozen kinds of imaging technologies exist, fMRI is currently perhaps the most important for cognitive neuroscience researchers. fMRI permits scientists to identify specific brain regions that are active when the subject is carrying out a task, such as reading a text, making a decision, or moving a finger. Scientists can thus compare the brain anatomy and activity of people who read well and poorly, or who make appropriate and inappropriate decisions. Much of what we've learned recently about cognition has been accomplished with fMRI technology.

Positron emission tomography (PET) is another important imaging technology. Scientists using PET insert a small amount of radioactively tagged glucose (or another appropriate compound) into the bloodstream of the experimental subject. Because glucose is the brain's principal food, the PET scans of subjects will reveal the brain areas with the most glucose (that are thus the most active) when, for example, the subjects are asked to say the first verb that comes to mind when they hear a specific noun—such as *cut* or *slice* when they hear the noun *knife.*

Emerging major advances in EEG technology may provide the best initial and potential venue for educational researchers. EEG is the least invasive, cheapest, and most portable of the imaging technologies. For example, because fMRI uses powerful magnets and PET uses radioactive isotopes, and both require expensive equipment in specialized laboratory settings, their use in educational research has been limited by ethical and financial considerations. Conversely, EEG measures electrical brain waves via electrodes placed on the skull, and so it's no more invasive than a blood pressure sleeve. Furthermore, the electrodes can now be placed inside a cap where they send wireless signals to a nearby computer, so a researcher could eventually observe brain activity in nonlaboratory settings, such as within a classroom.

Although we're excited about the potential use of imaging technologies in our understanding of many current cognitive mysteries and in the diagnosis and treatment of learning disabilities, worrisome issues exist. Imaging technologies can also become potentially superb lie detectors, and so their use and possible misuse in government, business, and our criminal justice system pose serious issues about the nature of privacy. For example, if police can't enter a suspect's house without a warrant, can they technologically enter a suspect's skull in search of evidence without the equivalent of a warrant?

Each recent technological and biological advance has brought both promise and concern. Brain imaging technology thus joins recent advances in genetics, medicine, and computer technology as another element of what promises to be an intellectually stimulating, challenging, and probably contentious era. See Figure 4.

See also Brain Waves

Brain Sciences

The scientific disciplines that focus on understanding the brain and its cognitive processes and that seek to remedy brain maladies.

Recent advances in research technology have helped the thousands of brain scientists to expand dramatically the type and amount of research discoveries and clinical applications. The number of specialized areas in the brain sciences is large and increasing, but the following four perhaps relate the most to issues that educators confront:

Neuroscience focuses on the scientific study of the nervous system's organization and development at both the cellular and systems levels. Its focus is more on research than on clinical applications.

Cognitive neuroscience focuses on how brain biology gives rise to emotion, attention, thought, and behavior. The term emerged in the late 1970s and is increasingly supplementing the term *psychology,* which historically was focused principally on behavior. Cognitive neuroscientists study many of the teaching and learning issues that are of importance to educators.

Neurology focuses on the medical diagnosis and treatment of nervous system disorders.

Psychiatry focuses on the medical diagnosis and treatment of mental disorders.

Brainstem

The finger-sized structure that relays sensorimotor information between body and brain and regulates such key survival functions as circulation, respiration, and endocrine gland activity. A collective term, it's composed of a number of specialized structures and nuclei within the hindbrain and midbrain. The back of the brainstem is connected to the cerebellum. See Figures 5–7.

See also Central Nervous System, Cerebellum, Hindbrain, Midbrain, Peripheral Nervous System, Reticular Formation

Brain Waves

The synchronized electrical patterns of cerebral cortex activity as graphed on paper via an electroencephalogram (EEG).

A brain's neurons are always active at some level, and electrodes placed on a skull can amplify and record oscillations in the activity of large populations of neurons. These oscillations are measured in the number of firing cycles or oscillations per second (one oscillation per second is a hertz [Hz]). Rhythmic firing patterns can vary from 1 Hz to 100 Hz. Certain rhythmic patterns have specific names and are associated with specific behaviors. This information can be used in the diagnosis of various brain disorders (such as epilepsy and multiple sclerosis) and in the study of cognition.

Alpha waves characterize a regular 8- to 13-Hz rhythm that occurs during a relaxed awake state with limited sensory input (eyes closed).

Beta waves characterize a smaller, faster, and less regular 13- to 30-Hz rhythm that occurs during an alert active state.

Gamma waves characterize a high-frequency 35- to 100-Hz rhythm that occurs during thinking. A wave pattern of 40 Hz has been associated with theories of consciousness.

Delta waves characterize a large, slow 1- to 4-Hz rhythm that occurs during deep dreamless sleep.

Theta waves characterize a slow 5- to 7-Hz rhythm that occurs during dreaming (REM sleep).

See also Brain Imaging Technology, Cerebral Cortex, Neuron, Sleep

Broca's Area (BRO-ka)

A region located in the lower back part of the (typically) left frontal lobe that is associated with the production of fluent spoken and written language.

French neurologist Paul Broca's 1861 discovery of the region provided the first proof of the localization of a brain function. Broca's area adjoins the section of the motor cortex that regulates face and hand activity (including speech and writing). People with Broca's aphasia can understand language but are severely limited in their ability to express it. See Figure 6.

See also Aphasia, Arcuate Fasciculus, Wernicke's Area

Brodmann Areas

The German neuroanatomist Korbinian Brodmann's pioneering way of organizing the cerebral cortex into distinct regions based on structural variations in neurons and on their organization within the cortex.

Brodmann identified 52 distinct numbered areas in 1909, and this system is still substantially used, although other scientists have further subdivided many of the original Brodmann areas into more than 200 areas. Brain imaging technology is now providing a better view of the functional organization of the cortex, where various cognitive tasks are processed. This specialization of cognitive functions into distinct brain areas is called *modularity.*

You could use a library as a model for the organization of the cortex, in that just as various shelf areas are dedicated to certain kinds of books (history, fiction, science, etc.), so are various cortex areas devoted to certain cognitive tasks (vision, reading, planning, initiating movements, etc.). Likewise, just as a student writing a term paper may draw information from materials in many library areas, so most cognitive activities are a collaboration of many brain areas. See Figures 6 and 11.

See also Cerebral Cortex

C

Catecholamine (cat-e-KOLE-a-meen)

A class of chemically related neurotransmitters that includes dopamine, epinephrine, and norepinephrine (or noradrenaline).

See also Dopamine, Epinephrine, Norepinephrine, Neuron, Neurotransmitter

Caudate Nucleus. *See* Basal Ganglia

Cell

The basic structural and functional unit of an organism. A cell is functionally composed of (a) a semipermeable membrane that encapsulates jellylike nutrient material (cytoplasm) and contains channels that allow for the selective in/out movement of nutrients and cell products; and (b) various processing and regulatory structures—principally, a nucleus that contains the cell's long, coiled, tightly packed DNA molecule that provides the genetic directions for protein synthesis. The human body has an estimated 100 trillion cells.

Various cellular processes regulate an organism's metabolism. They break down food into useful nutrients that they then use to construct body parts and provide our brain with the chemicals it needs. Related cells combine to form tissues and organs. Some of these multicellular systems serve structural or protective roles (e.g., bones, skin, fingernails, kidneys), some process nutrients (e.g., lungs, intestines, liver), and some move nutrients and information (e.g., blood vessels, neurons).

An entire body has functional parallels to a cell. Our body's version of a cell's semipermeable membrane is our 9-pound, 20-square-foot mantle of skin that keeps our insides in place, heat in, and infection out. A cell's membrane has channels that regulate the input and output of cellular materials, and our body has a selective sensory system that recognizes dangers and opportunities, selective digestive and genital systems that serve as in/out conduits for organic materials, and a language system that receives and sends psychological information.

The constant availability of nutrients is a problematic issue for both a cell and an organism, so both tend to take in more than they currently need. The excess is stored for later use—in cells as cytoplasm and in our body as fat and as nutrients circulating within our bloodstream. Our brain similarly organizes and stores experience as retrievable memories and potential problem-solving strategies.

Genetic nuclear processes (such as DNA and RNA) regulate cellular activity—principally maintaining the cell and building proteins out of nutrient materials that enter the cell and then distributing them appropriately for body use. Our brain is our body's equivalent of these cellular processes. It receives initially meaningless sensory information, organizes it into an integrated coherent model of what's occurring outside, and then determines an appropriate response.

A classroom similarly parallels this simple biological model. Its version of a cell's semipermeable membrane includes the walls, windows, doors, faucet, outlets, and so on, that encapsulate the inhabitants and regulate the in/out flow of students and information. Its cache of excess *nutrients* includes currently unused equipment and materials—and hopefully eager-to-learn students (think analogously of amino acids in a cell waiting to be organized into proteins so they can leave the cell and do something useful). The metaphoric equivalent of the cellular nucleus is the teacher, administration, and curriculum that combine to organize the school lives of students so that they will personally and intellectually move well beyond what they currently are.

What we thus have is a simple but excellent model used by biological systems from individual cells to social groups: a semipermeable membrane, an extensive collection of potentially useful but currently unorganized and unused materials, and an efficient organizing agent. Life itself! See Figure 1.

See also Amino Acid, Deoxyribonucleic Acid (DNA), Glia, Membrane, Metabolism, Neuron, Nucleus

Central Nervous System

The combination of brain and spinal cord. All danger and opportunity information that registers in or on our body travels to the spinal cord via the peripheral nervous system and then into our brain, where it's analyzed for a possible response. Cognitive decisions that require movement are sent from brain and spinal cord to the appropriate motor systems via the peripheral nervous system.

See also Nervous System, Peripheral Nervous System

Cerebellum

The relatively small two-hemisphere structure tucked under the cerebral hemispheres right behind the brainstem—the little bump at the lower back of our head.

The cerebellum is massively interconnected with the rest of our brain. Scientists long thought that the cerebellum's principal task was to coordinate automatic movement programs smoothly by modifying our brain's basic motor and balance decisions, but they now consider the cerebellum to also be an important support system for various other cognitive functions, such as to monitor and fine-tune unconscious sensory input (and especially touch).

Think of a computer-nerd friend who provides analogous support when you need to install some hardware or software or fix a glitch. You could probably do it by yourself, albeit awkwardly, but it's so nice to have your friend there to smooth your efforts— someone who understands the nuances in the instructions, who can easily and correctly connect things.

Cerebellum means "little brain" in Latin, but the deeply folded, elegantly organized, and densely packed cerebellum is 11% of our brain's weight, and about the area of one of the cerebral hemispheres when it's spread out. It also has more neurons than the rest of our brain.

The principal input into the cerebellum is processed by the 10 billion tiny granule cells, one of the smallest types of neuron in our brain (packed 6 million per square millimeter). Conversely, all cerebellar output is processed by Purkinje cells, one of the largest types of neurons in our brain. Three other types of neurons, stellate, basket, and Golgi cells, modulate the input/output activity of granule and Purkinje cells. See Figures 5–7.

See also Brainstem, Neuron

Cerebral Cortex

The outer deeply folded surface of the cerebrum that processes conscious sensory, thought, decision, and motor functions. The principal divisions of the cerebral cortex are the occipital, parietal, temporal, and frontal lobes and the hemispheres. (All these are discussed as separate entries.)

Our brain organizes its trillion-plus neurons and glial cells into (a) a relatively small subcortical area (the brainstem, cerebellum, and surrounding systems) whose modular structures innately regulate and coordinate such basic survival processes as circulation, respiration, and movement; and (b) the large surrounding six-layer sheet of deeply folded neural tissue called the cerebral cortex. The cerebral cortex encompasses 77% of our brain, and it processes learned rational behaviors that emerge out of the challenges we confront. The unfolded cortex is slightly larger than the size and thickness of a stack of six sheets of 12 × 18–inch construction paper.

The six layers of the cortex are principally populated by pyramidal and stellate (or granule) neurons. Pyramidal neurons have a pyramid-shaped cell body and long axon and dendrite extensions that extend well beyond their immediate cortical area. Star-shaped stellate (or granule) neurons have shorter axon-dendrite extensions and so connect principally with nearby neurons. Incoming information enters into Layer 4; internal processing of the information occurs in Layers 1 to 3; and the outgoing response leaves from Layers 5 and 6.

The cortex is principally composed of hundreds of millions of highly interconnected hair-thin (100-neuron) minicolumns that extend vertically through the six cortical layers (called the *gray matter*). Each minicolumn is specialized to process a very specific unit of information (such as to recognize a horizontal line or a specific tone). One hundred adjacent minicolumns combine into a unit to form a macrocolumn (about the thickness of the lead in a pencil) that can process more complex functions related to the minicolumns it incorporates (perhaps to help differentiate between the cello and flute version of a tone). Thousands of related macrocolumns form one of the 50-plus anatomically and functionally distinct Brodmann areas that each hemisphere contains.

The axons in columnar neurons extend down the column through the cortical layers into the *white matter,* a dense web of axon connections beneath the gray matter. The axons eventually leave the white matter to connect with dendrites in neurons in a related nearby column or to project into a column or brain nucleus elsewhere in our brain.

Thus, discrete columnar brain areas and systems process basic limited cognitive functions. These are incorporated into larger, specialized, widely distributed but highly interconnected areas and systems that collaborate on complex cognitive tasks. For example, our visual system has about 30 separate columnar subsystems that process such visual properties as shape, depth, color, quantity, and movement. The subsystem that responds to the color red processes it on every red object we see, and the subsystem that responds to circular shapes processes balls, compact disks, tires, donuts, and so on. Several of these subsystems will combine to process our perception of a single red ball rolling across a table.

Two simple metaphors will help your students understand the division and organization of our brain's hundreds of processing systems, many of which are innately dedicated to a specific important task—and most of which aren't active at any given time.

A Library Metaphor. Think of a 100-neuron column (in the gray matter) as containing the information in a 100-page book, and its axonal white matter (which connects with other neurons) as the bibliography that connects the information in that book to other books. Furthermore, think of the entire cerebral cortex as a library, the columns as library books, and the some 100 Brodmann areas that encompass the cerebral cortex as the various library areas (that contain books and other information on history, science, etc.).

Library shelf areas are thus assigned to a given category of books—fiction in one library area, science in another, and so on. A student would generally gather information from several books in a given area while preparing a report on that topic and would ignore library areas and books unrelated to the research topic. In similar fashion, our brain efficiently gathers the information it needs from brain areas specialized to provide the needed information or function and doesn't activate other unrelated areas.

Important library topics have more shelf space devoted to them than less important topics, but the library's shelf space can be reorganized to accommodate an expanding collection of books in a category. Dedicated (or modular) neuronal systems can similarly recruit neurons from less dedicated surrounding areas if they need more power to process their task. We can observe this developing spatial inequality in the larger amount of motor cortex space dedicated to coordinating movement in a person's dominant arm or hand compared with the other, or in the expansion of neuronal space devoted to left-hand digital capabilities when a right-handed person becomes a violin student.

A Kitchen Metaphor. A kitchen is a room where food is received, stored, and processed (and a brain similarly receives, integrates, and stores information arriving from inside and outside our body). A kitchen is filled with provisions and utensils suitable for a wide variety of menus, but most aren't being used at any given time. A cook planning to cook carrots uses only a peeler, knife, pan, water faucet, seasonings, and stove—not potatoes, the toaster, or other kitchen provisions or utensils. A recipe is a record of which out of many kitchen provisions and utensils are used to prepare the food (and a brain scan similarly records which brain areas are involved in an activity).

In a kitchen, a few key ingredients and utensils are used in almost all food production activity—food staples such as salt and onions, utensils for cutting and heating (and a few key brain systems and functions are similarly central to much of what we do).

Finally, kitchens often contain dull knives, broken equipment, and under- or overripe food that can affect the proper preparation of a menu (our brain can contain immature and malfunctioning systems that reduce the overall effectiveness of cognitive activity). See Figures 3, 5, 6, and 9–11.

See also Brainstem, Brodmann Areas, Cerebellum, Cerebral Hemispheres, Cerebrum, Frontal Lobes, Neuron, Occipital Lobes, Parietal Lobes, Temporal Lobes

Cerebral Hemispheres

The two major divisions of the cerebrum, separated by the deep longitudinal cerebral fissure into the right and left hemispheres and connected by the underlying corpus callosum and anterior commissure.

Most of our conscious thought and action are processed in the two cerebral hemispheres. They have different processing assignments but typically function as an integrated, efficient unit because they are so highly interconnected. Think, for example, of a couple who has determined the primary responsibility for each of various household tasks but who constantly discuss possible solutions to challenges that involve the family as a unit.

Responding to looming dangers and opportunities is an important cognitive task. The fundamental organizing principle for the right and left hemispheres emerges out of an important question a brain must answer before deciding how to respond to a challenge: Have I confronted this problem before?

The right hemisphere (in most humans) is organized principally to process novel challenges, and the left hemisphere to process knowledge and effective routines developed during previous similar challenges. For example, we process strange faces principally in our right hemisphere and familiar faces in the left. Musically naïve people process music principally in their right hemisphere, trained musicians in the left.

The initial solution to a novel challenge doesn't necessarily have to be the best solution—just something that works enough to keep us alive. We then save that solution as a memory, recall and edit it for use the next time we confront a similar problem, and then save that solution as a memory. Think of the similar way in which we save the successful drafts of a manuscript until it becomes just what we want it to be.

Although both hemispheres are active in processing most cognitive functions, the relative level of involvement shifts from the right to the left hemisphere over time and with increased competence. The right hemisphere is thus organized to respond rapidly and creatively to a novel challenge, but the more linear organization of the left hemisphere eventually translates the successful initial responses into an efficient established routine that is activated whenever the challenge reoccurs.

It makes sense. Grammatical language is an efficient, established procedure to enhance communication within a socially complex species, so it's not surprising that considerable left hemisphere space is devoted to it. A dependent infant uses whatever (right hemisphere) nonverbal communication skills he or she can creatively muster to get the help it needs but happily spends much of its childhood mastering the much more efficient existing cultural (left hemisphere) language template that we pass from generation to generation.

Each hemisphere is divided into four lobes. The three lobes in the back half receive and analyze incoming sensory information (occipital/sight, temporal/hearing, and parietal/touch) and integrate it into a perceptual map of the current challenges—the right hemisphere focusing on novel and the left hemisphere on familiar elements. The frontal lobe determines a response strategy—the right hemisphere again focusing on creative solutions to novel challenges, the left hemisphere on activating established routines.

We can thus think of the cerebral hemispheres as efficiently equipped to recognize (sensory lobes) and respond (frontal lobes) to novel (right hemisphere) and familiar (left hemisphere) challenges. See Figures 5, 6, and 9–11.

See also Cerebral Cortex, Cerebrum, Frontal Lobes, Occipital Lobes, Parietal Lobes, Temporal Lobes

Cerebrum

The combined right and left hemisphere regions in the large upper forebrain part of our brain. The cerebrum contains the top cerebral cortex layer of cells (gray matter) and the underling network of connections among cellular systems (white matter). Some brain scientists also include the diencephalon (thalamus, hypothalamus, pineal gland) as a part of the cerebrum, so it's somewhat confusing. See Figures 5 and 6–11.

See also Brain, Cerebral Cortex, Cerebral Hemisphere, Forebrain, Frontal Lobes, Hypothalamus, Occipital Lobes, Parietal Lobes, Temporal Lobes, Thalamus

Channel. *See* Neuron

Cholecystokinin (COLA-sis-toe-kine-in)

An intestinal peptide that helps to trigger the feeling of satiety after eating.

See also Neuron, Neurotransmitter

Cholinergic (ko-lin-UR-jik)

The term for neurons and receptors that use acetylcholine as a neurotransmitter.

See also Acetylcholine, Neuron, Neurotransmitter

Chromosome. *See* Deoxyribonucleic Acid (DNA)

Cingulate Gyrus (SIN-gyu-lat JY-rus)

An important integrative brain system that helps to reconcile ambiguous situations. It's located on top of the corpus callosum pathway that connects the two hemispheres and is connected to many brain systems.

The prefrontal cortex, which is massively interconnected to every brain and body system, has been called our brain's CEO (chief executive officer). We can think of the cingulate (and especially the anterior cingulate in the frontal lobe region) as an efficient executive assistant who schedules and expedites things and controls access to the CEO. The cingulate determines the emotional significance of incoming sensory information (from mere awareness to intense pain) and relays important information and related data to the prefrontal cortex for attention, decision, and action.

The cingulate is related to the amygdala in that the amygdala activates innate automatic responses to imminent fearful situations (fight, flight, freeze). But if the challenge is ambiguous or doesn't require an immediate response, the cingulate gets involved, consciously coordinating the retrieval and analysis of memories of responses to prior similar situations or the development of creative alternate responses for prefrontal cortex decision (or both). In effect, the cingulate helps us to *make up our mind* consciously about what to do when we confront ambiguous problems with several possible solutions. See Figures 7 and 8.

See also Amygdala, Corpus Callosum, Frontal Lobes

Circadian Rhythm

A biological activity rhythm of about 24 hours (Latin: *circa* means "about," *dies* means "day").

All plants and animals are affected by the moon's rotation around the earth. Although our awake/asleep periods tend to coincide with outside light and darkness, our circadian rhythms are actually regulated by an internal body clock within the hypothalamus (the suprachiasmatic nuclei), and its day is between 24 and 25 hours. We thus tend to reset our biological clock daily to meet the time demands of our society. We are most consciously aware of our awake/asleep cycle, but urine and hormonal production and body temperature are among the other functions that follow a regular circadian rhythm. Scientists have also discovered that the time at which a patient takes certain drugs can affect the efficacy of the drug.

See also Hypothalamus, Melatonin, Pineal Gland, Suprachiasmatic Nuclei

Circulatory System

Our body's pervasive tubular transportation system for moving nutrients, hormones, and waste matter within its 10-pint bloodstream.

To function as a living unit, the cells and systems that constitute our body must be able to communicate with one another. Our circulatory system transports nutrient and hormonal materials, and our nervous system transports information.

Our bone marrow, digestive system, and endocrine glands are the principal examples of systems that use fluid, tubular networks, and a pumping heart to transport their materials throughout our body and brain. They thus help to create a single interconnected functioning organism out of the widely distributed organs encased within the 20-square-foot mantle of skin that covers our body. The marrow and glands continually synthesize and discharge numerous red blood cells and hormones into the 60,000 miles of blood vessels that constitute our circulatory system.

Our circulatory system transports each blood cell or hormone molecule to any of numerous sites in our body prepared to receive it. It's a simple system that creates a whole body-brain response to a whole body-brain problem, such as "I'm hungry" or "I'm scared." Because it takes only a minute for each heartbeat of blood to move throughout our body, all the necessary organs quickly receive the nutrients and hormones they need to carry out their small part of the larger task at hand.

Think of this general distribution system as being functionally similar to a woman's plan to give a $10 bill to each of the first 12 red-headed people she meets while walking down a street. She knows she'll eventually hand out the bills, but she can't predict who will get them. On the other hand, if she wants to give $10 to a specific redheaded friend, it's more efficient to send it by direct mail than to walk the streets in the hope of meeting her friend before all the bills are gone.

The key functional difference between our circulatory and nervous systems is thus that blood circulation is a general and relatively slow distribution system, and neural transmission is a specific and very rapid distribution system. Like comparing newspaper ads and mail service, the issue isn't which distribution system is better, but which system is better for the specific task at hand.

Notice also the anatomic similarities between the two systems: circulatory system: input = veins; pumping function = heart; output = arteries. Nervous system: input = dendrites; processing function = neuron cell body; output = axon.

See also Hormones, Neuron

Classical Conditioning. *See* Conditioning

Cochlea (KOKE-lee-ah)

The snail-shaped fluid-filled inner ear structure that responds to sound waves via about 18,000 hair cells that convert various sound vibrations into nerve impulses that are relayed to the temporal lobe auditory cortex where hearing is processed. The inner ear also contains the vestibular apparatus that regulates our sense of balance. The Latin term for "snail shell" is *cochlea.*

See also Hearing

Cognition

The complex of activities through which a brain consciously acquires and processes information, determines a course of action, and acts (with language often playing important roles in this process).

Cognitive and Motor Degeneration

The incidence of dementia and movement disorders increases with advanced age, but trauma, strokes, and such illnesses as schizophrenia and Korsakoff's syndrome (acute alcoholism) can occur earlier in life and also result in serious cognitive and motor disabilities.

The "Big Three" medical problems have historically involved *external invasions* (infectious disease), *internal insurrections* (malignancies), and the inevitability of *death*. The medical profession has done quite well with invasions, seems to be progressing effectively with insurrections, and has increased our life span.

Unfortunately, this increase in life span has led to a greater incidence of age-related degenerative cognitive and motor maladies (such as Alzheimer's and Parkinson's diseases), long conventionally viewed as an unfortunate inevitable result of aging. The cost of caring for those who suffer serious cognitive or motor decline is enormous, however, and the impact on the family is typically devastating. We don't want our children and grandchildren to recall us as being incompetent at the end of a vibrant lifetime.

Death is inevitable, but it's in the public interest for scientists to seek solutions to cognitive and motor degeneration—at least to delay the onset and slow the progression. The goal is to live the highest-quality life possible until death finally looms.

What had seemed a hopeless quest a few years ago suddenly shows promise. The former belief of a static nonrenewable brain has given way to the concept of lifelong neuronal regeneration and plasticity. Furthermore, recent stem cell discoveries materially increase hopes that dysfunctional brain systems can be repaired and replaced through neuronal transplant. Dramatic developments are thus occurring in the medical treatment of many types of cognitive and motor disabilities and in the development of computerized technologies that can substitute for the inadequate cognitive or motor function.

Much of our cognitive activity focuses on movement—determining and predicting our movements and the movements of objects and others. Movement results from the expenditure of energy in space and time. Effective movements require efficient memory systems that encompass relevant factual knowledge about our environment (declarative memories) and motor skills that execute complex motor programs (procedural memories). Alzheimer's and Parkinson's diseases result from a deterioration of the cognitive systems that allow us to comprehend and navigate our space-time environment with ease.

The neurobiology of memory and motor loss as we age seems to result more from neuronal problems in our brain's lower subcortical areas (that synthesize many of our brain's regulatory neurotransmitters) than in the upper cortical areas (where many factual memory networks appear to be located). For example, Parkinson's disease results from neuronal loss in the subcortical substantia nigra, which synthesizes the dopamine that is highly concentrated in circuits that plan and process movement. The uncontrolled movements of Huntington's disease result from deterioration in the basal ganglia's caudate nucleus, which inhibits inappropriate movements. Alzheimer's disease results from neuronal degeneracy in the subcortical hippocampus, which plays an important role in long-term memory formation. Attention is obviously essential to learning, and the (principally subcortical) systems that process attention decline with age.

Research on cognitive and motor degeneration originally focused on the brain systems that regulate the processes. Recent dramatic developments in research technology now allow scientists to explore the minute molecular world of synapses (the connecting link between two neurons) as well, and this has led to the increased scientific optimism.

Such current research focuses on the roles of *signal molecules* (neurotransmitter systems, and especially glutamate), *growth molecules* (and especially nerve growth factor, a hormone that helps direct the establishment of neural networks), and *trophic molecules* (that provide the nutrition necessary to maintain the systems).

Those who have a family history of late-life cognitive/motor degeneration can feel reassured. Current research may not affect an aged loved one's longevity or quality of life, but it's very helpful to understand what's occurring within a patient's brain and reassuring to know that cognitive/motor deterioration isn't inevitable and will probably become treatable. Although degenerative pathologies can develop in anyone, it's especially important for older people to do what they can to maintain the health of their brain and body—to remain cognitively curious and active, to eat properly, and exercise regularly. See Figure 7.

See also Basal Ganglia, Dopamine, Hippocampus, Memory, Movement, Schizophrenia, Substantia Nigra

Reference

Black, I. (2001). *The dying of Enoch Wallace: Life, death, and the changing brain.* New York: McGraw-Hill.

Cognitive Neuroscience. *See* Brain Sciences

Conditioning

Forms of learning that are dependent on environmental stimuli.

Classical conditioning involves an initially neutral stimulus that subsequently will elicit a specific innate response after the two are repeatedly paired. Think of always using the same dish when you feed your dog. After a while, the dog will exhibit behavior consistent with food expectation whenever it sees you pick up the dish.

Operant conditioning uses reinforcement or reward (or both) to increase the frequency of the preferred response to a stimulus. Think of a situation in which you train your dog to walk in a circle and then reward that behavior with food. When the dog wants food, it will walk in a circle.

Conditioning theory originally didn't take phenomena such as interest and motivation into consideration. Humans frequently do things (such as to practice the piano) just because they enjoy them, and not because of some expected extrinsic reward.

Cone. *See* Sight

Consciousness

An enigmatic brain property that provides conscious organisms with a sense of self—a personal subjective awareness of one's own existence and that of the objects and events one confronts. Conscious organisms can selectively attend to a stimulus and temporarily hold information.

Consciousness abandons me when I go to sleep and magically reappears when I awaken. And when I'm conscious, I not only know something, but I know that I know it. So who is the "I" who is doing all this knowing? How is it possible for purely physical brain activity to lead to subjective experience? The search for the meaning and mechanisms of consciousness has historically been the speculative purview of philosophers and theologians (who often considered it a disembodied essence), but neuroscientists have recently begun to explore the biology of consciousness via the remarkable observational capabilities of brain imaging technology.

Conscious thought and behavior seem to emerge out of unconscious emotional arousal, which alerts us to potential dangers and opportunities and helps to activate an innate automatic response. If we have no innate automatic response to the challenge, unconscious emotional arousal can shift into conscious feelings, which activate relevant brain systems that can consciously and rationally analyze the challenge and develop a solution (albeit a solution often biased by the nature of our emotional arousal). Because school activities focus principally on conscious learning and behavior, understanding the biology of consciousness will be essential to the development of credible theories of teaching and learning. The renowned neuroscientist Antonio Damasio has proposed a three-part theory of consciousness that would be useful for such educational applications.

Protoself. In Damasio's theory, the biology of consciousness begins with a neuronal arrangement that maps every part of an organism's body into one of various interconnected brain areas. This mapping is necessary in all animals because brain and body must constantly communicate to maintain a continuously revised unconscious sense of what's happening throughout the organism.

A collection of automated brain systems that Damasio calls the protoself uses this continuous flow of information to manage various life processes, such as circulation and respiration. The protoself maintains the stability it needs across its lifetime by operating body systems within genetically established relatively narrow regulatory ranges.

Core Consciousness: The Present. We're conscious of more than our own self. Our protoself is imprisoned within the geography of its body, but sensorimotor and related brain systems also allow a conscious organism to explore the world. A stable body thus confronts a constantly shifting and expanding external environment.

So not only does a brain contain a map of its body, but a conscious brain must also have a mechanism for mapping and connecting to the external world. Damasio believes that consciousness emerges when the mapped relationship between an organism and an external object (which may be another organism) has risen to the level of a feeling of what's currently happening.

Core consciousness (which we share with many animals) is thus the consciousness of the here and now—a nonverbal imaged running account of the objects an organism confronts in a series of successive instants as it moves through and interacts with its immediate environment. Think of being both actor and spectator in a movie within our brain (a film being a sequence of still pictures that give the illusion of movement as they quickly pulsate through our brain).

Many catchphrases in our culture speak to the importance of recognizing and respecting the here and now in the quickly moving stream of consciousness that defines much of life ("Stop the world, I want to get off." "Slow down and smell the roses." "Seize the moment."). Core consciousness is primal in that it continuously focuses the organism on the immediate, which after all is where we live.

Extended Consciousness: The Past and Future. We may live in the present, but we have lived in the past, and we will probably live into the future. Damasio suggests that organisms must have a large cortex to move consciously beyond the here and now, to profit from past experiences and avoid potential problems. The cortex must be sufficiently large to contain a vast and powerful autobiographical memory that can quickly identify the largest possible range of information relevant to a novel challenge. Humans, and the great apes to a lesser extent, have such a cortex.

Intelligence emerges out of this ability to embellish and temporally extend core consciousness. It allows our brain to manipulate recalled information in the mental design and analysis of potential responses. The practical applications of conscious intelligence include imagination, creativity, and conscience, which led to language, art, science, technology, and a variety of cultural and political systems (such as the shared governance of a democratic society).

See also Cingulate Gyrus, Emotion and Feelings, Movement

References

Damasio, A. (1999). *The feeling of what happens: Body and emotion in the making of consciousness.* New York: Harcourt Brace.

Damasio, A. (2003). *Looking for Spinoza: Joy, sorrow and the feeling brain*. New York: Harcourt Brace.

Corpus Callosum (CORE-pus ka-LOW-sum)

A 4 × 1–inch band (or commissure) of myelinated axons that connects the related conscious thinking regions of the two cerebral hemispheres. Estimates range above and below 200 million axons, and some evidence exists that the commissures are larger in females than in males. The axons in each hemisphere emanate from Layers 2 and 3 and then project into Layer 4 in the opposite hemisphere.

Think analogously of a couple who have divided up household tasks but who constantly communicate before acting, and typically reach a consensus. The hemispheres represent the couple and the corpus callosum their constant communication.

In the 1960s, Roger Sperry and his associates severed the corpus callosa of patients who had intractable epilepsy. This reduced their seizures, but it eliminated their previous hemispheric communication. These people were extensively studied afterward, and this important research taught scientists much of what they learned about the hemispheric specialization of cognitive functions prior to the development of brain imaging technology. See Figure 7.

See also Anterior Commisure, Cerebral Hemispheres, Neuron

Cortical Columns. *See* Cerebral Cortex

Cortisol (KOR-ti-sol)

A hormone secreted by the adrenal gland into the bloodstream during stressful situations. Cortisol travels throughout our body and brain to activate various systems involved in fight/flight behaviors.

See also Hormones, Stress

D

Declarative Memory. *See* Memory

Delta Waves. *See* Brain Waves

Dementia. *See* Cognitive and Motor Degeneration

Dendrite. *See* Neuron

Deoxyribonucleic Acid (DNA)
(de-OX-ee-rye-bow-new-CLAY-ik)

A tiny, ladder-shaped, meter-long, twisted and folded, self-replicating molecule within the nucleus of every cell in an organism. All cells within an organism (except egg, sperm, and red blood cells) have identical DNA molecules. DNA helps to construct and maintain the organism, and it also transmits genetic information to subsequent generations of that organism.

Cells and organisms need a simple, efficient agent to organize their nutrient materials into the products and processes that help to define life. DNA and RNA (ribonucleic acid) carry out that function in a cell. Think of a cell as a kitchen, DNA as the genetic cookbook that contains recipes for all the proteins that a body can make, and RNA as the cook who reads the DNA recipe for a protein and then assembles it from the nutrient materials within the cellular cytoplasm. Just as a cook doesn't generally use all the recipes in a cookbook, so each cell assembles only a very limited number of proteins from the vast repertoire in our body's DNA.

The recipe for a protein is called a gene, a stretch of DNA that carries the coded information for assembling a protein. The human genome contains about 30,000 genes encompassed within 23 pairs of rod-shaped chromosomes. All proteins are made from only 20 different amino acids that can be arranged (or coded) into countless sequences and lengths, just as all 500,000 English words are made from only 26 letters that can be arranged into a great variety of sequences and lengths. The information in both proteins and words is not coded into the amino acids and letters themselves, but rather into the sequence of amino acids and letters and the length of the chain (as in *do, dog, god, good, goods*). Consider similarly the infinite number of melodies constructed from sequences of the 12 tones of the scale and our immense number system constructed from sequences of only 10 digits.

In *Genome: The Autobiography of a Species in 23 Chapters,* Matt Ridley suggests an intriguing hierarchical model of genetics, the Book of Life. Imagine the entire complement of human genes (our genome) as a book with 23 chapters (the number of paired chromosomes in the human genome). Each chromosome chapter is composed of several thousand protein stories called genes. Each protein story is made up of paragraphs called exons and introns (that play different roles in the synthesis of proteins). Each paragraph is made up of words called codons (each amino acid is represented in DNA by a distinct three-element code), and each codon word is made up of letters called bases (adenine, cytosine, guanine, and thymine make up the four-base genetic alphabet). The human genome is quite a book. Its 1 billion words are the equivalent of 800 Bibles—but the cell's nucleus that contains our entire genetic story would easily fit on the head of a pin.

We humans thus have a between-generations genetic code in which parents inform the next generation at conception how to construct and maintain a body (where to put the nose and arms, how to develop the brain, etc.). Then, when children are born, the parents use a related within-generation language code to teach them how to function effectively in a complex culture. The fundamentally similar functional organization of the two communication systems is both mysterious and amazing. Both create a complex communication system out of only a few elements (20 amino acids, 26 letters) because both coding systems insert the information into the sequence of elements and the length of the information chain rather than into the elements themselves.

See also Amino Acid, Language

Reference

Ridley, M. (2000). *Genome: The autobiography of a species in 23 chapters.* New York: Perennial.

Depolarization. *See* Neuron

Depression

A typically treatable mental condition characterized by general feelings of sadness and pessimism and by the lack of pleasure in things that most people enjoy.

Depression was long viewed as an adult illness, but 8% of adolescents and 2% of children are clinically depressed. Symptoms in young people include frequent but poorly defined physical complaints, deteriorating schoolwork, truancy, verbal outbursts, reckless behavior, loss of interest in friends, and high sensitivity to failure and social rejection. Because many adolescents periodically exhibit at least some of these behaviors, parents and educators often don't think in terms of clinical depression when such behaviors continue and increase. Adolescents who are depressed but not treated for it are at risk for drug abuse, social problems, eating and sleep disorders, and suicide (the third-leading cause of adolescent death).

The prevailing theory for depression centers on low levels of the neurotransmitter serotonin. Antidepressants such as Prozac, Paxil, and Zoloft reduce depression by increasing the effectiveness of brain serotonin. Recent studies have also implicated the neurotransmitters norepinephrine and dopamine in depression.

Depression affects about 5% of the population at any one time, and about 20% of the population suffers from it at some time in their lives. Compared with other forms of mental illness, depression seems to emerge more out of negative environmental conditions than genetic abnormalities.

See also Dopamine, Drugs, Norepinephrine, Serotonin

Development. *See* Growth and Development

Diencephalon. *See* Forebrain

Dopamine (DOPE-a-meen)

One of the class of catecholamine neurotransmitters. Dopamine is synthesized in the midbrain's substantia nigra and is sent into basal ganglia and frontal lobe areas where it helps to regulate emotional behaviors and conscious movements.

Low levels of dopamine are associated with Parkinson's disease, and high levels are associated with some forms of schizophrenia. Cocaine works in the dopamine circuitry. See Figure 5.

See also Catecholamine, Neuron, Neurotransmitter, Substantia Nigra

Dream. *See* Sleep

Drugs

A somewhat nebulous concept in that its basic definition—a chemical agent that in small amounts can significantly modify the way a body or brain functions—could include food, seasonings, and poison as well as heroin, prescription drugs, alcohol, and aspirin.

Sticks were probably among the first tools that we humans used in our long ascent to the complex technologies that have greatly extended our body and brain capabilities. The leaves or fruit of the bush that supplied the stick may also have provided the first drugs. Then as now, humans used drugs because they allow us to do things we otherwise couldn't do as easily, if at all.

Drugs have been an important part of human life for millennia, but until recently, we didn't know much about what they were or how they created their effects. Consequently, drugs took on a mystical character. People spoke of "magic mushrooms" and "reefer madness." Wine was the nectar of the gods. Drugs were incorporated into religious ceremonies and holiday celebrations. Experiences with drugs were both exciting and fearful, helpful and destructive.

Drug education programs emerged out of this general lack of understanding of the psychobiology of drugs, and so a strong moral tone dominated: Don't use drugs because they're harmful. Schools spoke of their drug and alcohol programs (as if alcohol were something other than a drug) or of having a drug-free campus (as if the coffeepots and soda machines were completely free of drugs).

Because our knowledge of the biochemistry and drug effects has now dramatically increased, school drug education programs should go beyond the moral overtones and end effects of drug use to a stronger focus on clear explanations of what drugs are, how they and their addictive properties work, and how to live intelligently with them. This shift will certainly rekindle the same argument used against sex education programs: If you teach students about sexuality (drugs), they will become sexually active (use drugs). Well, we've been teaching algebra to students for centuries and they don't rush out and do algebra.

Psychoactive Drugs. Neurotransmitter molecules produced within a *sending* neuron pass information to a *receiving* neuron at the synapse (the narrow gap between two neurons). The complementary shapes of the neurotransmitter and the receptor on the postsynaptic neuron allow them to bind (somewhat like a key and lock) and then to pass and receive chemical information.

The synapse is an area of constant molecular activity that would be chaotic without its simple molecular binding system. Think of a hotel with many people constantly entering, milling about, and leaving. Key codes and shapes ensure the correct match of patrons to rooms. The front part of the key contains the room's *address* and the back part the *information*—the patron holding it who can use it to enter the room. Anyone who holds the key or its duplicate has access to the room.

Psychoactive drugs are either plant or synthetic molecules that sufficiently resemble specific molecules involved in brain processes and can attach to the appropriate receptors. A psychoactive drug molecule enters our brain and a synaptic area through the bloodstream (which it entered after initially entering our body through respiration, digestion, or injection). Like a duplicate key, a drug uses its similar shape and chemical properties to attach to a presynaptic or postsynaptic receptor and to alter one of a variety of chemical actions that can occur in a synapse. For example, it can mimic the actions of a neurotransmitter that is typically released into the synapse, or it can alter the rate and quantity of neurotransmitter release, the shape and number of receptors, the strength of the action, or the ability of the presynaptic neuron to reuse its neurotransmitters.

The actions of psychoactive drugs can thus positively or negatively affect normal brain activity. Because the shape and chemical properties of drugs mimic those of brain molecules, drugs can obviously have positive effects, as exemplified by the widespread use of potentially dangerous drugs. Furthermore, drugs can stabilize the imbalances in neurotransmitter distribution that many people experience (for example, lithium stabilizes norepinephrine distribution patterns in people suffering from bipolar disorder).

Because drugs flood into the synapses of a brain area via the bloodstream rather than through the carefully regulated axon terminals of interrelated neurons, their heavy concentration and unregulated movements in and out of synapses can also negatively affect us—within the immediate brain region and in other parts of our body and brain. Thus, the caffeine that keeps us awake (and perhaps alive) during the final segment of a long, late drive home also will probably delay our desired sleep because the effects of caffeine persist over three hours. The small amount of alcohol that initially released our inhibitions in a social setting can, with increased consumption, trigger inappropriate behavior and uncoordinated movements. The morphine that reduces pain and enhances euphoria in addicts also reduces our brain's production of its own opiates, and so extends the addiction.

So psychoactive drugs are both helpful and harmful and almost always require a tradeoff. To maintain a quality life, our conscious brain must carefully control its drug selection and dosage, just as its unconscious partners in our skull and glands carefully control the production and distribution of neurotransmitters and hormones.

The brain mechanisms that respond to our environment's challenges mature during childhood and adolescence. Extensive drug use during this period can adversely affect this maturation, because drugs alter our brain's natural perception of and response to the environment. Thus, one drug may help keep us awake so that we can complete a task by its deadline, but another drug could destroy maturing neural networks that are critical to the problem-solving task. Drugs aren't good or bad per se. They are chemical technologies that positively and negatively affect the processing effectiveness of our biological brain. An effective drug education program should help students learn how to use their own biological resources to solve a problem and to use drugs only when that assistance is essential to maintaining an acceptable quality of life, realizing even then that many drugs have addictive properties that can reduce our ability to control their use.

Students need this kind of factual nonmoralizing information so that they can consciously learn to make informed conscious choices about what they put into their body and brain.

See also Hormones, Neurotransmitter

Dura Mater. *See* Meninges

Dyslexia. *See* Aphasia

E

EEG (Electroencephalography). *See* Brain Imaging Technology, Brain Waves

Emotion and Feelings

Emotion is an unconscious arousal system that alerts us to potential dangers and opportunities. Sufficiently aroused, it can activate conscious feelings about the challenge and bias the direction of its resolution. Subcortical brain systems process unconscious emotions, and cerebral cortex systems direct the processing of conscious feelings.

Think of emotion as a biological thermostat that monitors and reports variations from normality. If we don't have an innate reflexive response for a particular challenge, the emotional arousal will activate our attention system, which identifies the dynamics of the challenge and then activates relevant problem-solving systems that consciously respond to the challenge. Almost everything we do thus begins with emotion, a key cognitive process that was poorly understood for most of human history.

An ill-defined collection of structures called the limbic system was thought to regulate emotional arousal and processing during the second half of the 20th century, but that belief has come under increasing criticism. Emotion is so central to cognition that many if not most brain systems (including limbic system structures) probably participate in it. Emotion theory and research have recently advanced tremendously. The discussion that follows draws especially on the groundbreaking work of Antonio Damasio.

Emotions differ from feelings. Emotions unconsciously integrate sensory input from within and without and often publicly manifest themselves in facial, body, and speech displays. We can detect about 300 emotional expressions that the 44 human facial muscles regulate. It's often important that we inform others of the kind and severity of the challenge that confronts us. Emotional arousal can lead to conscious feelings that elevate our involvement with the challenge and so play a key role in the subsequent conscious design of our response. We typically hide our feelings from others, because it's often useful to not display what we plan to do.

Emotion researchers have identified a couple dozen discrete emotional states that exist along intensity continua, such as apprehension-fear-terror or annoyance-anger-rage. Some emotions are blends of simultaneously activated emotions, such as trust and fear creating submission or trust and joy blending into love. Although many researchers consider fear, anger, disgust, surprise, sadness, and joy to be the primary emotions, several classification systems have been proposed (just as in the various classifications of intelligences). Some emotional states imply social relationships—such as sympathy, guilt, jealousy, envy, and gratitude. Our processing system for emotions and feelings is thus complex.

Think of being in a state of current contentment (mental equilibrium, bodily homeostasis). Our sensory or memory systems (or both) detect an emotionally charged stimulus from inside or outside our body—a danger or an opportunity.

What follows is an immediate analysis of the relevant environment and the current state of our body and brain. The basic concerns: What are my current levels of alertness, strength, and energy? Are they such that I'm capable of successfully confronting the challenge—and further, am I motivated to do it? If the analysis is optimistic, various emotions and feelings that signal a joyful state will emerge (such as joy, anticipation, trust). On the other hand, if the analysis is pessimistic, emotions and feelings that signal a sadness state will emerge (such as fear, anger, grief). We'll thus move confidently forward in the design of a strategy that will resolve the challenge, or we'll warily avert it. Optimistic emotional/feeling states seem to be principally processed in the left frontal lobes, and pessimistic states in the right frontal lobes.

If the analysis doesn't clearly place us in either category, an uncertain emotional state results (surprise, confusion, and anticipation are relevant emotions for this state). The traditional fight-flight-freeze categories used to describe behavior in stressful situations thus also describe emotional arousal. We can often meta-cognitively sense this back-and-forth discussion going on in our brain while we're trying to decide on such things as a major purchase or what to do on a vacation.

These positive/negative emotional states often return after the fact, when we assess the results of our decision. Emotions such as elation and pride follow success, and shame and guilt follow defeat. The emotionally tagged memories of the experience pop up when subsequent similar challenges occur and can bias that analysis.

Our innate temperament can also bias the analysis and the resulting emotional state. Temperament emerges by the age of two and is generally categorized as either bold/uninhibited or anxious/inhibited. The bold tend to go toward challenges in optimistic curiosity, and the anxious tend to move away in pessimistic wariness.

Mood (which tends to exist over a shorter period, from a few hours to a few days) can similarly affect this analysis in the direction of the positive or negative mood we're experiencing. We may thus eagerly tackle a problem on Tuesday that we would avoid on Thursday.

Drugs, illness, and beliefs (religious, political, etc.) can also bias the accuracy of this analysis and the consequent conscious optimistic or pessimistic feelings that result. We may thus incorrectly feel that we're capable of meeting certain challenges, or vice versa.

What's emotionally true of an individual is also observable in social behaviors, such as fluctuating confidence levels in the stock market or in the body language and behavior of teams during a game. For example, basketball teams may have confident streaks during which they play very effectively, followed by an awkward period during which they suddenly seem to have lost confidence in themselves. Their body language often communicates their current emotional state and consequent level of play.

The social behavior that preceded the Iraq war paralleled what occurs within a single brain. The national and international debate that was sparked by a proposal for war focused on an assessment of our respective levels of alertness, strength, and energy—but also heavily on our motivation for the enterprise. How much will a war cost? How long will it take? How many will die? What will happen if we don't invade Iraq? What about the aftermath? Should we invade only if other nations join us in a coalition, or should we go it alone? *Should* we do it, even if we *can* do it?

The postwar analysis is as emotionally driven and perplexing as the prewar predictions. There's thus not much difference between an individual and a social group when it comes to the emotional analysis of a major challenge, and this is perhaps integral to our social nature. In this light, the arts and humanities often play an important arousal/focusing role in society that's analogous to the role that emotion/attention play in individuals. Picasso's mural *Guernica* and Aristophenes' drama *Lysistrata* are renowned examples of art forms that alerted (and continue to alert) society to culturally important dangers and opportunities—in both examples, to the horror of war.

Individually and socially, our emotions thus lead the way.

See also Anxiety, Limbic System, Stress, Temperament

References

Damasio, A. (1999). *The feeling of what happens: Body and emotion in the making of consciousness*. New York: Harcourt Brace.

Damasio, A. (2003). *Looking for Spinoza: Joy, sorrow and the feeling brain*. New York: Harcourt Brace.

Empathy

The ability to understand or to experience another person's emotional state and feelings, a property that emerges out of the childhood realization that other people are similar to us in many ways.

Sympathy differs from empathy because it's a kind-hearted recognition of the plight of another person without the sense of sharing that is central to empathy. Empathy is an important trait in that it leads to the ethical and altruistic behavior necessary in effective conflict resolution. Most children experience empathy in action when adults and playmates sense their joy or distress about something, respond appropriately, and discuss the situation with them. Explicit modeling of empathetic behavior at home and school enhances its development. Autism deprives a person of a sense of empathy.

See also Autism, Emotion and Feelings

Endocrine Glands (EN-do-krin)

The set of glands that secrete regulatory hormones into the bloodstream. Our brain's hypothalamus and its pituitary and pineal glands help to regulate the actions of our body glands (thyroid, parathyroid, pancreas, adrenals, and ovaries and testes).

Glands are organs that remove specific materials from the bloodstream and then either alter and secrete them for further body use (as with hormones) or excrete them from the body (as with urine). See Figure 7.

See also Brain, Hormones

Endorphin (en-DOR-fin)

The commonly used term for a class of peptides discovered in 1973 that reduce intense pain and enhance euphoria.

The endorphins are chemically and functionally similar to opium and morphine. Acupuncture, meditation, caressing, exercise, and positive social contact have been associated with elevated endorphin levels.

See also Neurotransmitter

Engram

A brain's physical manifestation of a memory—the set of neurons that fire when something is recalled.

Engram emerged as a concept and term when each memory was viewed as a discrete neuronal network (or trace) located in a specific brain area. Researchers today view memory and the editing and forgetting of memories as being much more complex than that, but the term persists.

See also Memory

Enzyme (EN-zime)

A class of substances that facilitate the synthesis of a new chemical by adding to or removing components in the existing chemical.

Epinephrine

Another name for adrenaline, typically when adrenaline is used as a neurotransmitter.

See also Adrenaline

Episodic Memory. *See* Memory

Evoked Potential

The electroencephalogram (EEG) measure of a brain's reaction to a specific sensory stimulus, recorded as a characteristic wave pattern.

When the stimulus is initiated by cognitive activity, it's typically called an event-related potential. An EP or ERP is symbolized by the letter P followed by the number of milliseconds the response pattern occurred following the stimulus. P300 is the typical response pattern to events that are unexpected, potentially important, or interesting.

See also Brain Imaging Technology, Brain Waves

Explicit Memory. *See* Memory

F

Fairness

The belief that all involved in an enterprise should participate and be treated equally.

When asked to list qualities they want in a teacher, students tend to give high ratings to a sense of humor and fairness, but they typically find it difficult to define either of these qualities. It seems a matter of recognizing something when we experience it without being able to define it precisely. Humor and fairness are thus complex social concepts with fuzzy, somewhat personal definitions.

Students realize and accept that schools contain two classes of people—adults responsible for administering the activities and students who engage in them. To students, fairness implies that the adults are diligent and effective in their work, just as adults expect the students to be in completing their assignments. Fairness further implies that adults treat students impartially in the distribution of resources, instructional assistance, evaluation, and interpersonal relations.

Students are generally willing to give some latitude to adults and schoolmates in periodic instances of unfairness, but an innate, principally frontal lobe system that matures through experience processes the key strategy for regulating reciprocity. The strategy is commonly called tit for tat: Cooperate with others on the first encounter, and then imitate whatever the other person does on subsequent occasions (or to modify the biblical injunction, *Do unto others as they have done unto you*). We see this at many levels, such as reciprocated Christmas card mailings that continue until one person drops the other or our tendency to quit patronizing a business that gave poor value but to give it another chance with a change of ownership.

Young children begin to develop tit-for-tat beliefs and behaviors and the ability to detect cheating in others through informal play with family and friends and by carrying out household tasks imposed by their parents (who can give or withhold favors). School provides a more complicated formal setting that introduces them to (a) a large nonkin group in a limited enclosed space, and (b) deferred rewards and punishments, such as within extended curricular projects and grades based on weeks of cumulated work.

Our emotional body language is quite transparent, so we become adept at detecting the subtle guilt signals that tit-for-tat cheaters often send. We similarly exhibit emotional displays that express our feelings to others about exchanges (for example, gratitude suggests fairness, and anger suggests unfairness). We tend to break off relationships that become untrustworthy.

Such experiences eventually move us toward a selection of personal friendships and business alliances with those we've come to trust. When a relationship reaches a sufficient level of trust through many successful tit-for-tat experiences, the parties often quit *keeping score* and (formally or informally) commit to an extended, more relaxed altruistic relationship. Marriage and collegial partnerships are examples of positive situations in which both parties can assume fair cooperative behavior and trust over an extended period.

Our complex society also requires a more abstract altruistic commitment—to do things for others with no hope of return (such as donating money to the poor or to charitable organizations that will probably never help us). Furthermore, we normally tip selected service employees (such as waiters and hotel maids) in businesses we may never return to, although we could usually get away with not leaving a tip.

Fairness is often codified into rules—in games, in classroom management, in institutional policies and procedures, in the marketplace, and in our legal system. It probably all begins with parental instructions on how to play and share toys with others, but it continues throughout life as a central element of how others view us.

See also Emotion and Feelings, Humor

Feelings. *See* Emotion and Feelings

fMRI (Functional Magnetic Resonance Imaging).
See Brain Imaging Technology

Forebrain

The upper and larger part of our brain, 75% of the weight of the central nervous system.

The diencephalon (lower part of the forebrain) contains the thalamus, hypothalamus, and pineal gland, which play key roles in the early processing of sensory information and in regulating the sympathetic nervous system. The telencephalon (upper part of the forebrain) is dominated by the cerebrum (cerebral hemispheres), which processes conscious thought and behavior, and the underlying basal ganglia, which provide key support for such cognitive activity. See Figures 5–11.

See also Anterior Commissure, Basal Ganglia, Brain, Central Nervous System, Cerebral Cortex, Cerebrum, Corpus Callosum, Frontal Lobes, Hindbrain, Hippocampus, Hypothalamus, Limbic System, Meninges, Midbrain, Motor Cortex, Occipital Lobes, Parietal Lobes

Fornix

An arch-shaped band of axons that begins at the hippocampus and serves as the principal pathway to the hypothalamus. See Figure 7.

See also Hippocampus, Hypothalamus

Frontal Lobes

The problem-solving, decision-making, action-initiating, paired lobes in the front part of the cerebral cortex (anterior to the central fissure), encompassing 41% of the cerebral cortex.

Imagine an ear-to-ear line across your skull. The sensory lobes of the cerebral cortex are principally located in the back (above the thalamus), and the frontal lobes are in the front (above the basal ganglia). The back-to-front organizing principle of both the cortical and subcortical areas is that the brain's back section recognizes and creates mental models of danger and opportunity challenges, and the front section manipulates and transforms these models into a response that it initiates. The basal ganglia process innate unconscious responses, and frontal lobes process learned conscious responses, but both systems participate in many decisions and behaviors.

The large human frontal lobes (and especially the prefrontal cortex directly behind our forehead) give us a distinct advantage in recognition and response activities because they allow us to move from the purely reactive behavior of most animals to being principally proactive—capable of consciously anticipating and preparing for potential novel and familiar challenges.

The prefrontal cortex is directly interconnected to every distinct functional unit of our brain, and so it coordinates and integrates most brain functions. The prefrontal areas are thus the functional equivalent of a corporate CEO or symphony conductor who coordinates and integrates the activities of many individuals. Like a good Internet search engine, the prefrontal cortex can quickly locate information necessary to decision making.

Two major frontal lobe pathways process foresight and insight functions. Foresight involves rational, logical thought processes—*how* to do something. Insight involves social skills and empathy—*whether* to do something. It should come as no surprise to parents of adolescents that foresight matures before insight. Adolescents can often successfully carry out inappropriate behaviors.

The importance of effective frontal lobes is further underscored by the growing awareness that many mental disorders (from attention deficits to schizophrenia) are associated principally with frontal lobe malfunction. See Figures 5–11.

See also Basal Ganglia, Cerebral Cortex, Cerebral Hemispheres, Cerebrum, Occipital Lobes, Parietal Lobes, Temporal Lobes, Thalamus

Fusiform Cell. *See* Spindle Neuron

G

GABA (Gamma-Aminobutyric Acid) (GAH-bah, GAM-ma a-MEE-no-bhu-TIER-ik)

An amino acid that also acts as a principal rapid inhibitory neurotransmitter in the brain and spinal cord. It's estimated that as many as one-third of all synapses in the cortex are GABA synapses. GABA plays an important role in circuits that regulate anxiety levels.

See also Glycine, Neuron, Neurotransmitter

Games. *See* Play and Games

Gamma Waves. *See* Brain Waves

Ganglion

A cluster of related neurons located in the peripheral nervous system that carries out a specific function. When such a cluster arrangement is located within the brain, it's called a nucleus.

See also Nucleus, Peripheral Nervous System

Gender

The separation of humans into males and females, with consequent cultural roles and behavioral expectations.

Gender similarities and differences and sexual orientation have become increasingly explosive issues—theologically, culturally, and politically. The issue is compounded by imaging research that can now compare male and female brain structures and cognitive activity in ways not previously possible and by the increasing awareness of intersexuality—a condition affecting up to 2% of children who are born with an ambiguous sexual system that later creates gender identity issues.

The traditional conventional wisdom that we consciously choose our sexual orientation has eroded as people thought more about their own personal experience and about other biological predispositions (such as handedness and temperament) that they similarly didn't consciously choose. The roles that culture and genetics play in gender behavior has similarly become problematic as parents observe developmental variations in children's play patterns and adolescent friendship preferences.

It thus appears that individuals are either clearly male or female, or else exist (for whatever biological or cultural reason) somewhere along an androgynous continuum between the two pure gender strains. Gender isn't the simple straightforward conscious phenomenon that most folks formerly believed, and that some folks continue to believe.

Some cultural gender differences seem to have little to do with biology, such as constantly shifting fashions and hairstyles, the division of household tasks, and the recent gender shift in professions—more women becoming medical doctors and attorneys, more men becoming nurses and early-childhood teachers.

Other differences are biological. It's obvious that different reproductive roles require related differences in male-female bodies and brains. For example, although the hormones testosterone, estrogen, oxytocin, and vasopressin are present in everyone, females typically have more estrogen and oxytocin, and males more testosterone and vasopressin. Furthermore, females have a monthly menstrual cycle, and males have both daily and yearly testosterone cycles (high morning and autumn, low evening and spring). The more complex question is whether other significant normative brain differences exist that aren't as easily related to reproductive roles.

The average male brain is slightly larger than the average female brain, but the average female brain is slightly larger if you factor in body-size differences. The corpus callosum that connects the two hemispheres is slightly larger in females, but the hypothalamic structure that seems to regulate sexual orientation is larger in males than in females (although at least some homosexual men have a female-sized structure). Females tend to have a more dominant left hemisphere, and males a more dominant right hemisphere. The significance of these and other differences is problematic and controversial.

Furthermore, our survival depends on our ability to understand how objects and systems function (systematizing capability) and to infer other people's thoughts and intentions (empathizing capability). Although males and females can do both adequately, males seem to have a slight edge in systematizing and females in empathizing. Memory involves recalling the general concept and also the factual knowledge that underlies the concept. Females seem to have an edge on factual recall and males on conceptual recall. Navigation strategies use geometric cues and the recall of landmarks. Males seem to depend more on geometric cues and females on landmarks. The typical male stress response is a fight/flight aggressive response, but in females it's often a tend/befriend nurturing response.

These and other reported gender differences create an interpretive dilemma. What we do know is that (a) males and females are structurally and behaviorally much more similar than different, (b) differences don't imply that one cognitive property or strategy is necessarily better than another, and (c) measurable differences must be interpreted in light of what's commonly called the *within/between factor* in normative research that compares group scores on human properties, capabilities, and behaviors (such as those listed here). The range of scores *within* each group is larger than the difference *between* the mean scores of the two groups. For example, consider height differences in large normally distributed male and female groups. The difference between the tallest and shortest person in each gender group will be greater than the difference between the average heights of the two groups of males and females. Thus, some females will be taller than some males in normative groups, even though the total population of males averages 7% taller than females.

Group differences only show group tendencies; they don't predict for any single person in either group. So although it's possible and appropriate to report general observations about male–female differences, it's inappropriate to stereotype—to use a general observation to bias one's perspective about the capabilities and behavior of an individual male or female. See Figure 8.

See also Hypothalamus, Stress

Gene. *See* Deoxyribonucleic Acid (DNA)

Glia

A vast system of support cells for neurons. Our brain has 10 times as many glial cells as neurons, and they comprise about half of the mass of our brain.

Although glia do not transmit the same kind of cognitive information neurons transmit, recent discoveries suggest that glia use chemical signals to affect both the synaptic communication among neurons and the formation of synapses. They thus play a far more significant role in learning and memory than formerly thought.

Glia means "glue," and glial cells were originally thought to be the glue that holds our brain together. In fetal brain development, star-shaped glial cells called astrocytes do act as a scaffolding of sorts that newly formed cerebral cortex neurons use in migrating from the subcortical region where they were created to the specific site in a cortical column and layer where they will carry out their appropriate neuronal function. Glial cells thus play a key role in establishing the general architecture of our brain. Think of glial cell extensions as the scaffolding of a *cortical* building, and the six layers of neurons that comprise the cortex as the floors, walls, furniture, and so forth, that are then attached to the scaffolding during construction.

Our brain must tightly control the chemical balance within its cells because chemical imbalances can result in mental illness. Glial astrocyte cells assist in this task by forming part of the blood-brain barrier that surrounds the capillaries, thus denying entry into our brain to many unnecessary or dangerous molecules that travel in the bloodstream.

Another type of glial cell, the oligodendrocytes, form an insulating layer called myelin around nerve fibers (axons) that send messages to distant cells, and this insulation increases the speed and precision of such neural messages. Multiple sclerosis is a disease that results from the deterioration of the myelin sheath.

Microglia are small glial cells that proliferate in response to injury in order to absorb damaged cells and any foreign bodies in the area. They thus serve a sort of immune system function.

Glial cells located in the peripheral nervous system have different names though similar functions. Schwann cells, like oligodendrocytes, create the myelin in peripheral neurons that surrounds both the axons and the synapses where the axon terminal and muscle meet. Satellite cells serve the same protective role as the microglia. See Figure 9.

See also Blood-Brain Barrier, Cerebral Cortex, Neuron

Glucocorticoid (GLUE-ko-KOR-ti-coid)

A type of steroid hormone that plays a key role in regulating a stress response.

When our brain becomes aware of a stressful situation, the hypothalamus activates the pituitary gland, which activates the adrenal glands, which secrete glucocorticoids such as cortisol into the bloodstream where they rapidly move to organs and tissues that participate in the stress response.

See also Hormones, Hypothalamus, Pituitary Gland, Stress

Glucose

A simple form of sugar (dextrose) that, along with oxygen, provides the energy neurons need to function.

Although essential to a functioning brain, glucose is not stored but must be continuously supplied through bloodstream nutrients. Glucose deprivation for 15 minutes will result in serious brain damage or death. Glucose emerges out of starch and sucrose during digestion and is stored in the body as glycogen. Hypoglycemia (and resultant dizzy sensations) results from low levels of glucose in the blood. Hyperglycemia (diabetes) results from high levels of glucose in the blood.

Some brain imaging technologies identify active brain systems through the higher concentrations of glucose in those brain regions.

Glutamate (GLUE-ta-mate)

An amino acid that also acts as a principal rapid excitatory neurotransmitter. It's been estimated that glutamate is the primary neurotransmitter in about half of our brain's neurons, and it appears to play an important role in processing vision, learning, and memory.

See also Glycine, Neuron, Neurotransmitter

Glycine (GLY-seen)

An amino acid that also acts as an inhibitory neurotransmitter. It's especially prevalent in the brainstem and spinal cord.

See also GABA (Gamma-Aminobutryic Acid), Neuron, Neurotransmitter

Glycogen. *See* Sleep

Granule Cells. *See* Cerebellum

Gray Matter. *See* Cerebral Cortex

Growth and Development

A measurable increase in size (growth) and the addition or modification of structures and functions (development).

A tree thus grows in size but develops new branches and leaves. Humans similarly *grow* in height and weight, but *develop* facial hair and breasts—and the ability to read and drive a car. We can modify some forms of growth (such as by cutting our hair and fingernails) and attempt to delay or accelerate normal biological development, but it's perhaps best to understand, follow, and enjoy the normal growth and development rhythms of life.

We're born with a very immature brain (about one-third of the adult size) because of our mother's upright stance and consequent relatively narrow birth canal. Our helpless beginning and long juvenile dependency prompted us to grow and develop into a cooperative social species with a rich, language-driven culture.

Social skills are thus developmentally important—and in our complex society, it's very important that immature children learn how to collaborate effectively with those who aren't kin, and who don't even share the values and traditions that are important to one's supportive family.

The early development of our self-organizing brain focuses on genetically driven, species-specific processing systems. Later development focuses on environmentally driven culturally specific processing systems. For example, our ability to speak is innate, but learning to speak a specific language is culturally specific.

We're born with a basic, survival-level version of most brain systems, and they function at that level with limited instruction and effort. Explicit instruction and extended practice mature such systems so that they can respond to more complex culturally driven challenges. A normal human ability range exists that limits response beyond this range to virtuosos and savants—and to the technologies that we develop to extend performance of the function beyond our biological capabilities.

We can divide our 20-year developmental trajectory into two periods of approximately 10 years. The developmental period from birth to about age 10 focuses on learning how to be *a human being*—learning to move, to communicate, and to master basic social skills and cultural information. Implicit in this is the childhood need to bond with protective kin—to learn and embrace the family rituals and traditions that constitute a family.

The developmental period from about 11 to 20 focuses on learning how to be *a productive reproductive* human being—planning for a vocation and exploring emotional commitment and sexuality. Implicit in this is the often distressing need of adolescents to distance themselves from family bonds, rituals, and traditions to explore those of the nonkin with whom they will spend most of their adult life.

The first four years of each of these two, decade-long developmental periods are characterized by slow, awkward beginnings preceding a normal move toward confidence and competence. For example, crawling leads to toddling leads to walking leads to running and leaping.

We tend to be far more indulgent of the inevitable developmental awkwardness and errors of young children than of related early adolescent awkwardness and errors. Demanding adults tend to forget that the mastery of something as complex as reflective thought or one's sexuality didn't occur instantly and without error in their life, and it likewise probably won't in their adolescent's life.

Competence during the first 10 years is characterized by a move toward rapid automatic responses to challenges. For example, slow, laborious initial reading tends to become reasonably automatic by age 10. Language includes the automatic mastery of a verbal taxonomy of generally accepted object, action, quality, and relationship categories. Similarly, morality and ethics include the mastery of a social taxonomy of culturally acceptable behaviors.

Competence during the second 10 years, however, is often appropriately characterized by delayed and reflective responses processed principally in the frontal lobes that mature during adolescence and early adulthood. For example, the common impulsive instant-gratification responses of a preadolescent become less impulsive as a maturing adolescent learns to explore options and social implications prior to making a response.

In effect, cognitive development during the first 10 years focuses on recognizing and understanding the dynamics of various environmental challenges (processed principally in the sensory lobes, which mature during childhood), and cognition during the second 10 years focuses on developing effective and appropriate problem-solving strategies for such challenges (processed principally in the frontal lobes, which principally mature during adolescence).

The cultural strategy for dealing with children with immature frontal lobes is to expect the adults in their lives to make many frontal lobe decisions for them—where to live, what to wear, when to go to bed, and so on. Children with immature frontal lobes are willing to let adults make such decisions. Infants who can't walk are similarly willing to let adults carry them. But just as young children generally don't want to be carried while they're learning to walk, adolescents don't want adults to make frontal lobe decisions for them while their frontal lobes are maturing.

The only way we can learn to walk is to practice walking, and the only way we can mature our frontal lobes is to practice the reflective problem solving and advanced social skills that our frontal lobes regulate—even though young people aren't very successful with it initially. Adolescence thus becomes a challenge for both the adolescents and the significant adults in their life.

Formal education follows this rhythmic 4-6-4-6-year developmental pattern. Children generally spend most of their birth to age four years in the (we hope) loving and indulgent confines of family life where basic motor, language, cultural, and social skills emerge. We then say, "You can do it with kin, can you do it with nonkin?" and move them into an elementary school with a couple dozen nonkin, where the curriculum focuses on more complex motor, language, cultural, and social knowledge and skills.

The 11–14 middle school years embrace the initially awkward emergence of adolescence. The middle school and preschool years are thus developmentally similar in that they both represent the initial awkward development of important brain systems and cognitive functions: sensory lobe recognition capabilities during the preschool years and frontal lobe response capabilities during the middle school years.

The high school and early college years are similarly related to the elementary school years: the maturation of sensory lobe capabilities between ages 5 and 10 and the maturation of frontal lobe capabilities between ages 15 and 20.

See also Language, Music, Play and Games, Problem Solving

Gyrus (JIE-rus)

Any of the many external ridges in the deeply folded cerebral cortex.

Think of a gyrus as a hill and its corresponding sulcus as a narrow valley between two close hills. Crumble a sheet of paper to demonstrate how a large surface area can be compressed into a small space through such convolutions. Perhaps the best-known brain gyri are the angular gyrus and cingulate gyrus. See Figure 9.

See also Angular Gyrus, Cerebral Cortex, Cingulate Gyrus, Sulcus

H

Habituation

An element of learning in which repeated exposure to a stimulus decreases the strength of the response.

In habituation, the stimulus hasn't changed, but the brain eventually realizes that the stimulus is nonthreatening or unimportant, and so basically ignores or merely monitors it. Habituation is the opposite of sensitization, in which the brain rapidly identifies a stimulus as threatening or important, and so increases the level of its response.

Hearing

A sensory capability that recognizes and locates the source of sound variations.

Hearing and vision are the only sensory modalities that allow us to locate the source of the stimulus. Unlike our eyes, our ears have no protective lids that also shut out stimuli. Hearing is thus a 24-hour monitoring system that can pick up potentially important information from behind a wall, in the dark, or across a relatively large distance. Furthermore, our auditory system can focus on what's important and ignore currently unimportant sounds—a phenomenon experienced in a noisy social setting when we suddenly hear our name or some other emotionally loaded word in a nearby conversation and immediately shift our attention to it.

Hearing is a three-phase action that creates useful cognitive information out of the pitch, volume, and timbre of complex overlapping sound waves that vibrate through air, bone, and fluid. The process begins in our outer ear, where striking sound waves vibrate our eardrum. Our middle ear increases the strength of these vibrations about 22 times through the mechanical actions of the three smallest bones in our body (commonly called the hammer, anvil, and stirrup). They relay the increased vibrations to the cochlea, a fluid-filled tube in the inner ear that's shaped like a snail shell. Each of the about 18,000 hairlike receptors in the cochlea is tuned to a specific sound frequency. If the sound waves moving through the fluid bend a receptor, it activates a neural message at a specific frequency that's sent via the appropriate auditory nerve's 30,000 axons to our brain's auditory cortex within the temporal lobe.

The auditory nerve thus contains more than one axon for each of the cochlear receptors, whereas the visual information processed by 127 retinal rods or cones is compressed into one axon in the optic nerve tract. These different ratios may explain why our visual system mixes yellow and blue to get green, but our auditory system hears all the notes in a chord. Like the optic nerve, the auditory nerve runs through our brain's sensory relay center in the thalamus and divides so that both ears connect with the processing centers located above both ears.

Much human hearing involves processing phonemes and integrating them into language. A child's auditory system can normally recognize sounds that are only 10 milliseconds apart—1/100 of a second. Because stop consonants (such as b, p, k) require 40 milliseconds and vowels require 100 milliseconds, a normal auditory system can easily separate and process the various phonemes that constitute a word, and so such children's phonemic systems mature quickly in the welter of words they constantly hear. Conversely, children with language learning delay (LLD) have an auditory system that can recognize only sounds that are maybe 250 milliseconds apart (a quarter of a second), so words are just jumbled sounds to them. Speech development and reading thus become seriously delayed. Recent dramatic advances in the diagnosis and treatment of these problems optimistically suggest that many current language disorders will eventually be alleviated.

Our brain can recognize about a half million sounds across 10 octaves, but it can't process all possible sounds (such as very soft sounds). We distinguish between pleasant and unpleasant sounds, music and noise, but such judgments are often quite personal. We have many kinds of music and musical instruments, and our 3,000 human languages vary somewhat in the sounds they use, but all human music and languages use the same basic set of sounds—an example of human unity within nature's complexity. See Figure 6.

See also Cochlea, Phoneme, Retina, Sight, Wernicke's Area

Hemispheres. *See* Cerebral Hemispheres

Hindbrain

The small (2% of brain volume) bottom part of our brain that connects with the spinal cord.

Also known as the rhombencephalon, the hindbrain relays sensorimotor information between body and brain and regulates such key unconscious processes as heart rate, breathing, and level of alertness. Principal structures include the lower part of the brainstem (medulla oblongata, pons, reticular formation) and the cerebellum. See Figures 5 and 7.

See also Brainstem, Cerebellum, Forebrain, Locus Ceruleus, Midbrain, Reticular Formation, Sleep

Hippocampus (hip-po-KAM-pus)

A pair of curved structures under the inner surface of the temporal lobes that play a key role in the formation and retrieval of long-term declarative memories (which seemingly are stored elsewhere in the cerebral cortex).

Hippocampus is the Greek word for "seahorse," which the hippocampus somewhat resembles. Much of what scientists initially learned about memory and amnesia came from a man called HM whose hippocampus was almost entirely removed during a surgery to reduce the effects of his epilepsy. He was unable to form new declarative memories after the surgery. Similarly, Alzheimer's disease involves the progressive degeneration of hippocampal neurons, and of declarative memory functions. See Figures 6 and 8.

See also Amnesia, Memory, Temporal Lobes

Histamine (HISS-ta-mean)

A monoamine neurotransmitter that operates in brain areas that regulate emotion and allergic reactions. Its circuitry is similar to norepinephrine.

See also Neuron, Neurotransmitter

Homunculus (ho-MONK-you-lus)

A term for two common cartoon figures of a person in which the body parts are drawn in proportion to the amount of somatosensory or motor cortex space devoted to them, rather than to the proportional amount of space they actually occupy in our body.

For example, our body is mapped along the motor cortex, and relatively little space is devoted to our large trunk, which has few muscles, but much motor cortex space is devoted to our physically smaller hand and mouth areas because these are the most complex muscle systems in our body and so require large neuronal areas to process them. The motor homunculus depicts these disparities.

Homunculus is a Latin term meaning "little man," and so the term also refers to the incorrect folklore belief about consciousness that the psychological equivalent of a little man who *sees* retinal images and *hears* cochlear sounds resides within our brain (and seemingly another little man resides within the first little man, and so on). See Figure 10.

See also Motor Cortex, Somatosensory Cortex

Hormones

Chemical messengers synthesized in endocrine glands and secreted into the bloodstream that travel to target cells in brain and body systems that must respond to an internal or external challenge.

Because hormones travel through the bloodstream, they function within a time frame of minutes compared with the millisecond time frame of neuronal transmission.

Most hormones are classified as either steroids or peptides. Ring-shaped steroids (such as cortisol, testosterone, and estrogen) are synthesized in the adrenal cortex, testes, and ovaries; are made of cholesterol; and bind to receptors inside a target cell. Peptides (such as oxytocin, vasopressin, and growth hormone) are synthesized in the other endocrine glands, are short amino acid chains, and bind to receptors on a cell's surface.

See also Cortisol, Endocrine Glands, Neurotransmitter, Oxytocin, Stress, Vassopressin

Humor

Amusement and possibly laughter that result from the controlled ambiguity of an unexpected nondestructive event.

When asked to list qualities they want in a teacher, students tend to give high ratings to a sense of humor and fairness, but they typically find it difficult to define either of these qualities. It seems a matter of recognizing something when we experience it without being able to define it precisely. Humor and fairness are thus complex social concepts with fuzzy definitions. Let's focus, therefore, on perhaps the most educationally significant element of humor.

A teacher's sense of humor involves more than simply telling jokes. Rather, it often seems to deal more with the ability to pleasantly signal that current behavior is approaching the edge of what's considered normal or acceptable.

We're a social species, functioning principally within a normal range of biologically possible and culturally appropriate behavior. It makes sense. The biological cost-benefit ratio would be too high for a life span and behavioral capabilities that go well beyond our current normal ranges. Similarly, a social species must behave within an appropriate cultural range if it's to collaborate successfully on survival and reproductive tasks.

Young people frequently push at the edges of what's possible and appropriate, because they'll never truly understand normality if they don't discover where it ends (the Olympics being our periodic formal search for selected physical limits). Because young people often lack the experience and maturity of self-assessment, they expect others to help let them know—albeit with *a sense of humor*—when they've gone too far.

Think of a behavioral continuum that ranges from abnormally negative to abnormally positive. We all need to know how others view our behavior along this continuum. As our behavior moves toward and into the abnormally negative, others typically let us know with an escalating sequence of responses from simple frowns to outbursts of anger, disgust, and alarm. At the positive end, the sequence shifts from smiles and gentle encouragement to effusive joy and praise.

As suggested earlier, we could thus view an important, much-appreciated element of a teacher's sense of humor as being a pleasant nonthreatening technique for letting students know that they're moving toward *the edge*. The teacher inserts an appreciated noncritical smile prior to a frown—intonation and body language communicating that "everything's OK for now, but I'm watching you." This gives the student a chance to consider whether to proceed.

Students also appreciate the verbal and body language that communicates the teacher's early awareness of behavior that's just beginning to move toward the positive edge of the continuum. It's initial but escalating encouragement to go further, beyond the normal range. Its smile communicates, "I know you can do it, go for it!"

The term *kidding* is often positively associated with a teacher's sense of humor. Sarcasm isn't. To be effective, the indirect body language and intonation of kidding must imply a genuine love of and respect for the person being kidded, even though the actual words may suggest negative connotations.

Young children often can't correctly interpret kidding. Our right frontal lobes appear to process the verbal and affective discrepancies that play an important role in humor (and thus in kidding). The immature frontal lobes of young children can't process subtle categorical discrepancies (such as in the puns and word play of kidding). They tend rather to enjoy the humor of broad discrepancies (such as in slapstick humor). Adults thus tend to be direct when advising young children and more indirect with adolescents. Middle school students are typically caught in the developmental middle.

Humor often results in laughter, an ill-understood instinctive contagious emotional outburst that can both bond and humiliate people. Positive laughter has the potential to enhance both the health of individual students and group cohesion. In effect, it communicates, "We all understand what's occurring and it's at *the exciting edge.*" It's thus not surprising that students intuitively appreciate teachers with the sense of humor that creates a joyful nonthreatening classroom that's often encroaching the edge. The students perhaps can't precisely define the concept, but they certainly do appreciate its ability to reduce the negative feelings of anxiety and stress they would otherwise experience.

See also Fairness

Hydrocephalus (hide-row-SEFF-ah-lus)

An excessive amount of cerebrospinal fluid that leads to an enlarged skull and other medical and mental problems in infants.

Hydrocephalus is commonly called "water on the brain." It is a result of a blockage in cerebrospinal fluid circulation, and so it can also occur later in life because of trauma, infection, or tumor.

See also Ventricle

Hyperpolarization. *See* Neuron

Hypothalamus (high-po-THAL-ah-mus)

A cherry-sized collection of many key brain nuclei that directly and indirectly regulate body functions in response to internal and external conditions.

Often called *the brain's brain,* the hypothalamus is located in the center of things—behind our eyes, below the thalamus, above the pituitary gland, and connected (via the fornix) to the hippocampus. It seems to be connected to and involved in everything—body temperature, blood circulation, hunger and thirst, sleep, sexual arousal, hormonal secretion, and fight/flight responses. The combination of thalamus, hypothalamus, and pineal gland is called the diencephalon. See Figures 7 and 8.

See also Fornix, Hippocampus, Nucleus, Pineal Gland, Pituitary Gland, Thalamus

I

Imaging Technology. *See* Brain Imaging Technology

Immune System

The system of structures and substances that defends our body against antigens (bacteria, viruses, fungi, pollutants) that can enter our body, and helps to repair the damage they cause if they do enter.

We live in a complex environment replete with dangers and opportunities. Two highly interconnected internal systems recognize and respond to such challenges: (a) Our skull-centered brain, composed of more than a trillion highly interconnected neurons and glial support cells, integrates and responds to information that our sensory system can process; and (b) our diffused immune system, composed of an equally immense number of (often free-floating) cells spread throughout our body, responds to the several pounds of invisible microbes that typically inhabit our body, destroying those that are dangerous.

So our very interconnected brain responds to the larger visible external challenges, and our very diffused immune system responds to the tiny invisible internal challenges. A successful response to many of life's challenges requires the collaboration of the two systems and their endocrine gland system partner.

Illness can occur if they don't. Asthma and multiple sclerosis are examples of immune disorders in that the immune system can't properly differentiate between body tissue and foreign substances. Furthermore, the immune system is depressed during extended periods of stress, and this can lead to infections our body would otherwise fight off.

See also Brain, Endocrine Glands, Stress

Implicit Memory. *See* Memory

Insula

Two thumb-sized, pyramid-shaped structures deep within the folds of the two cerebral hemispheres that help process several important functions, such as feeling pain, processing taste, translating unconscious emotions into conscious feelings, and sequencing speech movements.

See also Cerebral Hemispheres, Emotion and Feelings, Taste

Intelligence

A somewhat nebulous concept related to the nature and assessment of a person's ability to respond successfully to challenges and to learn from such experiences.

Intelligence had long been thought of as a combined cognitive property that could be quantified and appropriately placed somewhere along a scale of general intelligence that uses 100 as an average score for a given age (IQ; intelligence quotient). During the final 25 years of the 20th century, the concept of multiple intelligences emerged—a belief that intelligence encompasses rather a number of separate cognitive abilities and that the current challenge determines the combination that will be used to resolve it. Furthermore, a person's competence level could vary among the various intelligences (such as to possess both exceptional musical ability and below-average mathematical ability).

Scientists can now use imaging technology to study brain activity in subjects who are carrying out tasks that require intelligent response, and so we can anticipate an enhanced understanding of intelligence. One interesting counterintuitive discovery is that subjects who are considered quite intelligent in an area actually use less brain energy to solve problems in that area than the less intelligent. So intelligence may involve the rapid efficient use of existing effective neural networks rather than an extended inefficient search for a solution.

Educators have embraced the concept of multiple intelligences, because it relates well to the way formal education is organized. Several theories have emerged, but Howard Gardner's theory of multiple intelligences is probably the best-known theory in educational circles. Gardner currently proposes eight forms of intelligence that focus on one's ability to successfully process key identity-space-time elements of human life. *Intrapersonal* and *interpersonal* intelligences reflect one's capabilities with the personal and social elements of problems. *Spatial, bodily-kinesthetic,* and *naturalist* intelligences reflect one's capabilities with the space-place elements of problems. *Language, musical,* and *logical-mathematical* intelligences reflect one's capabilities with the temporal-sequential elements of problems.

Robert Sternberg proposed a triarchic theory of intelligence. *Creative intelligence* involves the cognitive processes that identify and formulate good problems and ideas, question existing assumptions, and overcome obstacles in developing new ways to do things. *Analytic intelligence* involves the cognitive processes that consciously solve well- or ill-structured problems, make intuitive and reasoned decisions among choices, and judge the quality of ideas. *Practical intelligence* involves the action-oriented cognitive processes developed principally through experience that help us to analyze challenges effectively as we confront them in everyday life, and then to use this information to solve such problems—the term "street smarts" comes to mind.

David Perkins views intelligence as distributed within our brain and culture through various human and machine interactions, affected by the cognitive overload of our complex culture, dialectic in its multiple approaches to problems, and meta-cognitive, in its self-awareness of its own cognitive behavior.

Perkins sees intelligence as encompassing three elements: *Neural intelligence* involves the quantity, quality, speed, and precision of our various innate brain systems. *Experiential intelligence* involves specialized early and useful context-specific experiences. *Reflective intelligence* involves reflective regulation of our knowledge, skills, and attitudes—in effect, knowing *our way around* various knowledge and skill realms that define human life.

References

Gardner, H. (1983). *Frames of mind: The theory of multiple intelligences.* New York: Basic Books.

Perkins, D. (1995). *Outsmarting I.Q.: The emerging theory of learnable intelligence.* New York: Free Press.

Sternberg, R. (1996). *Successful intelligence: How practical and creative intelligence determine success in life.* New York: Simon & Schuster.

Interneuron

A class of short-axon local neurons that connect nearby brain areas and pathways (compared with neurons that connect to distant brain areas or to our sensory and motor systems).

See also Cerebral Cortex, Neuron

K

Knowledge. *See* Belief and Knowledge

Korsakoff's Syndrome. *See* Cognitive and Motor Degeneration

L

Language

An innate human capability that uses a system of meaningless sequential sounds and written symbols to communicate meaningful feelings, thoughts, and planned actions to other humans and to enhance inner thought processes. Although language is processed principally in the left hemisphere in most people, it's a complex process that at some level actively engages almost all of our brain.

Primates such as chimpanzees communicate at an intimate level through a behavior called grooming in which they clean the hair and skin of another chimpanzee. They also have an innate system of about three dozen vocal signals that alert the total group to various dangers and opportunities (such as predators and food), each signal having a specific meaning (danger overhead!) that is seemingly understood in infancy.

Humans similarly use touching and caressing as an intimate communication tool, and we similarly have vocal communication systems of several dozen phonemic sounds (44 phonemes in English) that we can use to communicate with individuals or groups. We've also added a written equivalent that in English uses 26 letters.

A major difference between primate and human communication is that we've turned a few dozen meaningless phonemes (and letters) into a meaningful language of 500,000 words by adapting the particle principle used to construct chemical compounds and proteins. The principle is that a relatively small number of stable particles—atoms, amino acids, or phonemes—can be hierarchically assembled into an infinite number of complex combinations. Thus, 20 amino acids and 44 phonemes can be assembled into myriads of proteins and words because the information in proteins and words is not coded into the amino acids and phonemes themselves, but rather into the sequence of amino acids and phonemes and the length of the chain (such as in the words *do, dog, god, good, goods*).

Consider similarly the infinite number of melodies constructed from sequences of 12 tones and our immense number system constructed from sequences of only 10 digits.

Primate communication is thus very limited, and human language is limitless.

Most children easily learn the common words that represent objects and events in their life (semantics). The words within a sentence similarly follow a preferred sequence that enhances meaning (syntax). By the time they enter school, most children have developed an adequate vocabulary, have informally mastered the syntactical conventions of our language, and can correctly string sentences into interesting conversation and stories (discourse).

Language proficiency thus begins with an auditory system that can hear speech sounds and an innate phonological module in the child's brain that can rapidly process speech—separating heard words into their phonemes, and then combining phonemes into spoken words. Most children can recognize sounds that are 10 milliseconds apart, and because stop consonants (such as b, p, k) require 40 ms and vowels require 100 ms, a normal auditory system can easily separate and process the various phonemes in a word. The phonemic systems of such children thus mature quickly in the welter of words they constantly hear.

Speech comprehension and production are unfortunately delayed in children with an impaired phonological module that can process only sounds that are more than 100 milliseconds apart. Their module simply won't become robust in a speaking environment if most words are processed as jumbled noise and not discrete phoneme sequences. The problem gets worse when these children enter school and are expected to automatically associate the 26 letters of our written alphabet with the 44 phonemes that they have yet to master. Most of their classmates are up to the challenge, but it is at this point that children with dyslexia historically begin their long slide into despair.

Spoken language emerges almost effortlessly for most, but written language requires our brain to go a step further and associate meaningless sequences of vertical-horizontal-diagonal-curved lines with spoken language, so written language requires extended explicit instruction. Even competent readers don't master reading and writing as easily as they mastered speaking.

Successful developments involving early diagnosis and intensive interventions with children who have language-processing difficulties are creating an optimistic belief that almost all children will soon be able to master the central human capability for oral and written language. See Figure 6.

See also Agnosia, Aphasia, Broca's Area, Deoxyribonucleic Acid (DNA), Hearing, Music, Phoneme, Wernicke's Area

Lateral Geniculate Nucleus. *See* Thalamus

Lateralization

When a cognitive function is primarily located in one of the two cerebral hemispheres.

Some functions, such as language and handedness, are predominantly processed in one of the cerebral hemispheres. About 90% of humans process language primarily in the left hemisphere, and the right hemisphere area of the motor cortex band processes movements on the left side of the body (and vice versa). Despite such functional asymmetry, the two hemispheres collaborate at some level in almost all cognitive functions.

See also Cerebral Hemispheres, Language, Motor Cortex

Learning

How our brain acquires new information and skills that persist, as differentiated from memory, which refers to how and where our brain stores learned information and skills.

Although scientists have long studied learning and memory, they still have an incomplete understanding of the neurobiology of the functions—but they're optimistic that brain imaging research will spur dramatic advances in such understanding.

Current knowledge suggests that learning involves the development of new or more robust neuronal pathways and synaptic connections, and the appropriate distribution of relevant neurotransmitters. Learning is enhanced when an experience is emotionally loaded or repeated, and learning a skill is especially dependent on repeated practice.

Learning disabilities can result from the developmental delay or traumatic or diseased loss of one or more relevant neuronal pathways and systems or from an over- or underdistribution of relevant neurotransmitters. Behavioral interventions help the learning disabled if the problem involves strengthening nonrobust pathways, and chemical interventions help those with neurotransmitter deficiencies.

See also Memory

Lesion

A specific damaged or diseased area of a body or brain. A lesion can be experimentally induced to study its effect.

Limbic System

An ill-defined ring of interconnected cortical and subcortical structures surrounding the brainstem, long thought to regulate emotional activity and memory.

Although the term is still popularly used as a simplification for the processing complexity of emotion and memory, no general agreement exists about which structures make up the limbic system or how they collectively process emotional arousal and memory. Structures commonly included in the limbic system are the amygdala, hippocampus, hypothalamus, fornix, cingulate, and septum. The Latin term for border is *limbus,* and limbic structures do border the inner surface of the temporal lobes. See Figures 7 and 8.

See also Amygdala, Cingulate Gyrus, Fornix, Hippocampus, Hypothalamus, Septum

Locus Ceruleus (LOW-kus sir-RULE-ee-us)

Brainstem nuclei that synthesize and secrete the neurotransmitter norepinephrine and that initiate REM (rapid eye movement) sleep and its consequent muscle paralysis. See Figures 5 and 7.

See also Brainstem, Norepinephrine, Sleep

Locus of Control

A person's belief about the relationship between an event and what caused the event. Those with an internal locus of control believe that events that affect them are typically the consequences of decisions they have made. Those with an external locus of control believe that fate, luck, and the decisions of others are typically responsible for events that affect them. Most people function somewhere between the extremes of this continuum.

See also Belief and Knowledge, Emotion and Feelings

Love

An intense joyful attraction between two people that typically leads to romantic and familial bonding. The term is also commonly used in a broader personal sense, such as an individual's love of sports, music, food, students, books, or God.

We've long associated love with our heart, but it really encompasses our entire body and brain, our entire psychological being, our entire life span, and researchers are now unlocking many of its mysteries. Romantic love (and perhaps other forms of love) appears to follow a three-stage lust-attraction-attachment sequence that emerged out of our strong biological drive to reproduce and our need to nurture children over their extended developmental period. Couples in love who have no plans for children apparently also follow the same biological sequence.

Scientists can now use brain imaging technology to identify the specific brain and chemical systems that drive the process. The hypothalamus, caudate nucleus, nucleus accumbens, septum, and several frontal lobe areas are especially active when love is on our mind, and dopamine, norepinephrine, serotonin, endorphin, oxytocin, vasopressin, testosterone, and estrogen are molecules that seemingly jump for joy. So it's party time all over our body and brain when love is in the air.

Lust begins the initially abstract process with testosterone and estrogen providing an encouraging push to just go looking. Pheromones and personality predispositions probably assist in narrowing the field (such as eliminating close relatives). Sometimes skyrockets go off immediately, and sometimes things heat up slowly—but biological lust leads to psychological attraction.

Attraction is highly focused attention. One's beloved becomes foreground and absolutely everything else becomes background. This is a time for fine-tuning initial impressions, and so the couple spends hours checking out each other. If the attraction remains mutually supportive long enough to resolve any nagging concerns, the third stage of attachment kicks in.

Attachment is for the long haul, because it must maintain the relationship though inevitable distractions. Oxytocin, vasopressin, and endorphins become part of the bonding glue that maintains the relationship whenever temporary troubles arise. An additional, often-helpful cultural glue involves such things as wedding promises before family and friends, joint ownership of possessions, and children who need parental nurturing.

Children typically enter into a loving relationship with their parents at Stage 2 attraction—the soulful gazing into a parental face, the oxytocin boost from nursing, the cuddling behavior that elevates oxytocin, vasopressin, and endorphin levels in both parent and child. Children have to fall in love with their parents and their parents have to fall in love with them. Mother Nature sees to it that they typically can hardly resist each other—until puberty, when lust kicks in, and they have to go looking elsewhere to help continue their species' biological destiny.

Love is obviously more complex than this, and it encompasses many issues of appropriateness and legality that currently confront our culture. Some folks think that reducing love to neurochemicals activating brain systems demeans the concept of love, but I think not. How wonderful to realize that falling and staying in love involves a perhaps forever-mystical synchronization of two biological systems—and that's what the poets and song writers have basically told us all along.

But how wonderful also that human love is so multidimensional, encompassing such a broad range of capabilities and possibilities. The biochemical complexities of love allow people who are infertile or homosexual to fall in love and yearn to rear children, and people who have lost a partner through death or divorce to fall in love again. People are willing to teach, nurse, and coach the children of others. Two people who have few friends and seemingly no prospects will suddenly discover each other. Love is such a marvelously adaptable human property!

School is an important institution in a child's life for many reasons, but being in daily contact with a room full of nonkin peers is especially important. It gives students many opportunities to observe the range of human values and behavior, and so to begin the complex extended process that will lead to attraction and attachment.

See also Gender. All the brain areas and chemical systems listed here are discussed elsewhere in this book in their own entries.

M

Magnocellular. *See* Sight

Medulla. *See* Brainstem

Melatonin

A hormone synthesized and secreted by the pineal gland. It helps to regulate our sleep and circadian rhythms, and so can affect mood.

Melatonin is synthesized from serotonin in the pineal gland. Increases in melatonin levels bring drowsiness and sleep. It's normally produced during the evening and night hours and used up during the day, so people who live in northern climates may suffer from a condition called seasonal affective disorder during the long winter months when days are short. *Jet lag* is a related short-term problem in which one's normal day is lengthened or shortened by rapid flight across several time zones. A form of jet lag affects many early adolescents as they go through the hormonal adjustments of puberty. It's like they're psychologically living two time zones west of where they actually live—going to sleep and waking later than they formerly did despite secondary school schedules not tuned to their current sleeping–waking cycles. See Figure 7.

See also Circadian Rhythm, Pineal Gland, Serotonin, Sleep

Membrane

A thin lipid (fatty) double layer that covers cells and so maintains their structural integrity. The membrane's fatty nature keeps it from dissolving within its watery environment and separates the different watery fluids inside and outside the cell. A semipermeable membrane (such as in a neuron) contains pores through which some substances but not others can enter and leave a cell. We can also think of our skin and the outer layer of organs as membranes. See Figure 1.

See also Cell, Neuron

Meme

The cultural equivalent of a biological gene.

A *gene* contains and transmits the cross-generation biological information an organism needs to develop and maintain itself. A *meme* is the cultural equivalent of a gene—a bit of replicated information that spreads through a society via imitation, teaching, and learning. Memes can range from trivial jokes, tunes, and slogans to such useful information as how to acquire and prepare food and shelter. Like genes, memes can evolve over time (such as in clothing fashions) and pass from one generation to the next (such as through books, films, recordings).

Animals that have a relatively short life span and live within a narrow ecological niche are born with innate survival and reproductive strategies. They typically die when they confront an environmental challenge beyond their innate capabilities. Variant members of their species that can somehow meet the challenge will survive, and so pass on the genetic characteristics that enhanced their success. The concept of *learning* for such species is thus principally an evolutionary process in which subsequent generations gradually adapt to environmental change.

Humans need a supplementary strategy. We have a long, interdependent life span and can live almost anywhere. We thus confront many complex challenges that would be impossible to encode genetically (such as recognizing individuals, recalling restaurants, playing a piano, and constructing clothing). Because we're born with an immature brain, most of our survival strategies aren't innate, but must be learned throughout life, and especially during our extended juvenile stage. Brain processes that enhance learning are thus essential to human life. Mirror neurons, memory, and memes are key elements of this complex system.

Memetic information is probably stored in memory networks where it's principally used while solving personal problems, but it can also be transmitted to others via imitation and language. It's also possible that many people will store a specific meme within the same or related brain location and configuration.

A memory network is a neuronal configuration that can represent an idea, object, or event. Think of the *Happy Birthday* song. A birthday will activate the memory network, but it's also possible for other networks in our brain to trigger the network internally, even though no birthday is being celebrated (and you're probably mentally singing the *Happy Birthday* song right now).

Yet just as it's possible to construct a protein by *expressing* the information in a gene without destroying the gene in the process, it's similarly possible to transmit the information in our memory into other brains via language or behavior without destroying our own memory. It's a replication of information, not a gift. The *Happy Birthday* song thus becomes a meme whose evolutionary travels among culturally related brains are analogous to the spread of genetic information within a species.

See also Memory, Mirror Neurons

References

Aunger, R. (2002). *The electric meme: A new theory of how we think.* New York: Free Press.

Blackmore, S. (1999). *The meme machine.* New York: Oxford University Press.

Memory

How and where our brain stores learned information and skills that can be retrieved (as compared to the concept of learning, which refers to how our brain acquires information and skills).

Although scientists have long studied learning and memory, they still have an incomplete understanding of its neurobiology—but they're optimistic that brain imaging research will spur dramatic advances in such understanding.

A memory of something seems to be diffused among a variety of related brain modules, each specialized to process a constituent element of the memory (such as a color, shape, pattern, label, or location). The various brain modules that constitute a memory are physically linked; so activating one memory element will activate others (such as being able to visualize someone when you hear her voice on the phone).

We thus don't have to store an infinite number of complete discrete memories that exist like a photograph, but rather reconstruct a triggered memory from a huge store of highly interconnected reusable elements developed from our life experiences. For example, the part of our visual system that recognizes the color red will respond to anything red, such as exit signs, stoplights, and catsup. If seeing a doll triggers a woman's memory of a favorite one from childhood, the shape, face, color, and texture processing systems that the sight of the current doll activated will also activate the connected feature and emotional memories of her childhood doll. We could thus think of memory as something that exists only when it's needed to connect current with previous experiences.

Scientists generally divide memory into several systems: (a) a short-term/limited-capacity element of our attention system called working memory (or working brain) that has no long-term recall and (b) a more complex, two-part long-term memory system that unconsciously processes skills (procedural memory) such as knowing how to touch-type, and that consciously processes factual label-and-location information (declarative memory).

Scientists further subdivide declarative memory into autobiographical memories of personal experiences (episodic memory) such as our memory of learning how to type, and cultural memories of more abstract and symbolic objects, events, and relationships (semantic memory) such as of knowing the common names and elements of word processors. We further tend to remember when and where specific episodic but not semantic learning activities took place. For example, I remember studying spelling in elementary school, but I don't remember when I learned to spell *accommodate* correctly.

Because emotional arousal activates the attentional focus that may lead to learning and memory, we create separate emotional memories that help to spark such activation (and a subcortical almond-shaped structure called the amygdala appears to play an important role in processing emotional memories). Think of factual memory as being more about remembering *what happened,* and emotional memory as being about remembering *how I felt about what happened.* Both are important, but our emotional memories are the more powerful. For example, our emotional memories of childhood are stronger than our remembrance of all the factual details of childhood.

Factual memory formation and recall requires emotional time and space associations with the various elements of a perceived object or event (such as whether a history fact will be on the test). A factual memory is thus tied to its context and so is easily learned and forgotten. If school requirements are the only context for the material to be learned, it's easily forgotten when we leave school—as all of us have experienced as students. Students often misbehave when they are required to learn things that have no context for (or emotional relationship to) their personal lives.

Use the following memory metaphor to help students understand the important functional relationship between our emotional and factual memories.

When we're overwhelmed by information or challenge, we tend to reinvent the related body/brain process outside of our body and let that technology carry the load. Examples include phone books, dictionaries, calculators, and photographs. Thus, in our search for a simple explanation for emotional and factual memory, it's useful to metaphorically explore the systems outside of our skull that we've developed to store and retrieve complex combinations of information.

The combination of file cabinet, file folders, and files is a useful metaphor because it has many functional parallels to what our brain actually does as it gathers, organizes, stores, retrieves, and uses information.

Think of your brain as a reasonably full and useful file cabinet. Think then of an emotional memory as a file folder (within a cabinet drawer) that contains many files—the factual memories of specific objects and events related to the emotion. When you pull out a file folder, you have easy access to all the files within it. When the file folder is in the file cabinet, though, you don't have easy access to the files.

It's useful to limit ready access to many of our factual memories to contextual situations in which we're in the time, space, and emotional *neighborhood.* Imagine a trip to the downtown area of a city you've visited, but not recently. Before going, you may have trouble recalling specific locations, stores, cafés, and so on, but when you arrive in the area, many factual memories easily return. The emotional state of being there automatically pops out the relevant file folder, and you have ready access to the factual information you need.

Imagine the cognitive overload if we had continuous easy access to all such factual memories even when we didn't need them—when we weren't in the neighborhood? Or think of how we effortlessly recall long-dormant memories of people and events while attending a class reunion, or the instant recall of prior related negative experiences during an argument with a spouse or friend.

We thus have the best access to strong emotional memories (the file folders), which then provide easy access to related but weaker factual memories (the files). Factual memories without emotional context are difficult to store and retrieve. The names, dates, and places kinds of curricular information we ask students to remember are a good example. Students often ask, "Will this be on the test?" and if the answer is "Yes," they then have a useful *emotional file folder* for the class information: POTENTIAL TEST ITEMS. During the test, they'll psychologically pull out and use the file folder and its names, dates, and places information—but as indicated earlier, alas, it's quite uncertain whether the file folder will ever come out in any nontest situation.

School simulation and role-playing activities thus provide a useful emotional context (or file folder) because they are related to real-life emotional uses of the information. Conversely, multiple-choice (and related) tests generally mask the context of factual information. The result is that students often associate the facts with the test rather than with their cultural utility. Students who pass the test may still be unable to retrieve and use the information in its cultural context.

If the emotional overtones of an experience are important, we may create especially strong emotional and weak factual memories of the event. Thus, an abused child who must continue to live in an abusive situation may be better off focusing on aversion strategies than on remembering all the details of past abuse. A strong related emotional stimulus years later may then trigger the recall of these weak factual memories (something that can also occur with long-dormant school memories at a class reunion).

Even if we don't already have an emotional file folder for an issue we confront for the first time, we tend toward an almost immediate emotional response that elicits a memory (such as when terrorists used passenger planes as guided missiles to destroy New York City's World Trade Center on September 11, 2001). Think of the organization of a library. If the book we seek is gone, we usually examine the two adjacent books, because libraries are organized so that the two adjacent books are always the closest in focus and content to any shelved book. Similarly, when we confront a novel challenge, our emotional system tends to begin our response sequence with something we consider metaphorically similar. In the case of the World Trade Center attacks, perhaps the concept of religious martyrs or the World War II Japanese kamikaze pilots popped up in your mind.

See also Learning

Meninges (me-NIN-jees)

The three protective connective tissue layers that cover and so encapsulate the brain and spinal cord. The layers from the inside out are called the pia mater, arachnoid mater, and dura mater.

Our body is covered by a 9-pound, 20-square-foot, pliable, protective skin membrane, but our brain is so vulnerable to external damage that it is additionally covered by the three meninges and

29 fused bones of our skull. Think analogously of the meninges as a protective and supportive *underwear* layer between brain and skull.

The singular form of meninges is *meninx,* the Greek term for "membrane." In Latin, *pia mater* means "tender mother" and *dura mater* means "hard mother"—and the dura mater is indeed the tough, thick, fibrous outer covering of the meninges. Cerebrospinal fluid between the transparent arachnoid mater (Greek for "weblike") and the thin transparent pia mater cushions our brain against blows to the head and intense head shaking.

Meningitis is a bacterial infection that results in an inflammation of the meninges. Tumors that exert pressure on the brain may develop in the meninges. See Figure 5.

See also Forebrain, Membrane

Metabolism

The biological processes through which organisms use nutrients and cellular mechanisms to regulate the growth and development of body parts and energy.

Microglia. *See* Glia

Midbrain

The middle part of the brainstem—about 4% of our brain's volume. Also known as the mesencephalon, it helps relay sensorimotor information between body and brain, regulates reflexive visual and auditory behaviors (such as blinking and pupil dilation), and through its substantia nigra plays an important role in regulating movements. See Figure 5.

See also Brainstem, Forebrain, Hindbrain, Substantia Nigra

Mirror Neurons

Neurons in the premotor cortex and possibly elsewhere that activate both when observing a specific action in another person (such as a smile) and also when carrying out the same action. They are the neuronal substrate of mimicry.

The development of a smoothly controlled motor system is a major childhood priority. Suckling is almost the first mobile act of an infant, followed by the brain-outward maturation of the arm and leg systems—eating before grasping before walking. Because mobility is a central human characteristic, these innate systems must develop early at the survival level without formal instruction. This motor development includes specific currently ill-understood periods during which various key specialized brain systems generally develop (such as walking at about one year, talking at about two years).

How infants begin their mastery of complex motor behaviors is a fascinating developmental phenomenon. Consider a behavior that most parents observe. If you stick out your tongue to an observant infant shortly after birth, the probability is high that she will reciprocate the behavior.

Sticking out our tongue is an uncommon act for humans, and it requires the activation of a complex motor neuron sequence. Our tongue is an important muscle system that facilitates eating and speech, so we normally keep it inside our mouth. An infant could randomly fire the appropriate motor neurons for tongue projection, but that's not what occurs when an infant sticks out her tongue in immediate mimicry of a parent's action. How can an infant possibly master such a complex motor act immediately after observing it?

The remarkable *mirror neuron* system explains the modeling-mimicking process that is central to much human learning. Initial studies focused on a left hemisphere area that regulates speech production in humans (Broca's area). The discovery of mirror neurons might provide the same powerful unifying framework for our understanding of teaching and learning that the discovery of DNA did for our understanding of genetics.

A smoothly coordinated motor sequence involves the typically unconscious preparation for a movement followed by the actual movement. For example, while my left index finger is typing the *c* in *cat*, my left little finger is getting ready to type *a* and my left index finger will shortly move up to the top row to type the *t*. The result is a single seamless typing action—*cat*.

The motor cortex plays a key role in activating such muscles. It's a narrow ear-to-ear band of neural tissue, with specific segments dedicated to regulating specific groups of body muscles. The premotor area directly in front of the motor cortex primes the next movements in a motor sequence.

Neurons in the premotor area that fire in preparation for upcoming movements also fire when we observe someone else carry out that action. Common brain regions thus process both the perception and production of a movement. The infant's observation of her parent's projecting tongue fires the premotor neurons that represent her tongue, and this priming activates the related motor cortex neurons that project her tongue out in mimicry.

We experience this mimicking phenomenon most commonly when we see someone yawn, and then typically have to stifle our own. Because infants must learn many movements, they don't inhibit the mimicking of movements they observe. For them, it's "monkey see, monkey do" (and it's interesting that the initial mirror neuron research was done on monkeys).

Our mirror neurons won't fire at the mere observation of a hand or mouth—only when it's carrying out a goal-directed action. Furthermore, they will respond to a hand but not to a tool that's grasping or moving an object (because body parts and not tools are represented in our motor and premotor areas).

Mirror neurons may thus facilitate the preliminary motor neuron simulation, priming, programming, and rehearsing that occurs in children, and this process obviously enhances our eventual mastery of complex motor behaviors and our ability to "read" the minds of others. For example, inferring the potential movements of others is an essential skill in many games in which players try to fake out opponents. Mirror neuron stimulation may also explain why so many people enjoy observing the movements of virtuoso athletes, dancers, and musicians. It allows us to represent actions mentally that we can't mimic physically. Note the related active body language of former athletes as they observe a game they once played.

Scientists are also exploring the relationship between mirror neuron activity and our ability to imagine our own planned actions, be empathetic, and develop articulate speech. Mirror neurons may thus eventually help to explain many teaching and learning mysteries in which modeling provides children with an effective behavioral pattern to follow; they may also help to explain disabilities (such as autism) in which children can't "read" the minds of others.

Children denied the opportunity to observe and thus develop a motor-driven survival skill that they would normally master with ease during its preferred developmental period may not recover from the deprivation. A good example is the tragic case of Genie, who was 13 when discovered hidden naked in a closet. Her mentally disturbed parents had almost totally deprived her of normal language and motor development. Competent therapists who then tried to undo the damage were only marginally successful (Rymer, 1993).

Mirror neurons may well become this century's equivalent of the mid-20th-century discovery of DNA. See Figures 6 and 10.

See also Frontal Lobes, Motor Cortex

References

Meltzoff, A., & Prinz, W. (2002). *The imitative mind: Development, evolution, and brain bases.* Cambridge, England: Cambridge University Press. (Note especially chapter 14 by the principal discoverers of mirror neurons, Giacomo Rizzolatti and Vittorio Gallese, "From mirror neurons to imitation: Facts and speculations," pp. 247–266).

Rymer, R. (1993). *Genie: An abused child's flight from silence.* New York: HarperCollins.

Mitochondria (my-toe-KON-dria)

Bean-shaped cellular organelles that contain a form of DNA inherited only from the mother's egg. Mitochondria are the principal source of energy generation within cells. See Figure 2.

See also Cell, Deoxyribonucleic Acid (DNA)

Modularity. *See* Brodmann Areas

Mood. *See* Emotion and Feelings

Motor Cortex

A narrow band in the posterior part of the frontal lobes (just in front of the somatosensory cortex) devoted to the initial conscious generation of precise body movements.

Think of a two-inch-wide band stretching across the top of our brain from ear to ear—the left side regulating the muscles on the right side of our body, and the right side regulating the muscles on the left side of our body—and we're represented upside down. The areas at the top of our brain regulate the foot muscles, and the areas by our ears control the facial muscles. The amount of motor cortex space devoted to a part of the body is related to the complexity and precision of its movements and not to the size of the body part. The face and hands thus received the most space because of the complexity and precision of their movement patterns. The premotor area directly in front of the motor cortex primes the next movements in a motor sequence.

The basal ganglia and the cerebellum are two other important elements of our movement regulation system. See Figures 6 and 10.

See also Basal Ganglia, Cerebellum, Frontal Lobes, Homunculus, Mirror Neurons, Movement, Somatosensory Cortex

Movement

A central function of our brain, and of our very existence.

The renowned evolutionary theorist Stephen J. Gould suggested that we're inside-out crustaceans. A crustacean's skeleton is on the outside, ours is on the inside. Our soft tissue and appendages are out where we can readily observe them.

Having an internal skeleton means that we have a direct, intimate, sensory knowledge of how our three-part external motor system functions—feet and legs, hands and arms, and mouth and face. From birth on, we can observe and feel muscular contractions and their relationship to body movements. We've created many tools (such as stopwatches and tape measures) that accurately measure the properties of our marvelous movement system. Furthermore, we've always celebrated this basic universal understanding and awe of our motor system through performance and competition.

Well, why not? Our motor system is perhaps *the* definitive element of our biological self. Compare the two major biological groups, plants and animals. Plants don't have a brain, and animals do. Plants don't have a brain because they're not going anywhere—and if you're not going anywhere, you don't even need to know where you are. What's the advantage for a rooted tree to realize that other trees are better situated, or to be able to observe approaching loggers?

On the other hand, if you have legs, wings, fins, or other appendages that permit mobility, you need a sensory system to tell you about here and there. Then you need a make-up-your-mind system to decide if *there* is better than *here,* or *here* is better than *there.* Finally, you need to activate your motor system to move to *there,* if you've decided it's better than *here.*

We spend much of our extended juvenile development period informally observing and exploring our motor system. We have to learn how to regulate and predict its movements and the movements of others (and of moving objects). It's a complex system that must be activated for thousands of hours to reach the adult proficiency levels of complex movements. We've turned much of this juvenile practice activity into enjoyable play and games.

Our mobility systems can even get us beyond direct physical movement. For example, our vocal apparatus can rhythmically move air molecules that hit the eardrums of others at a distance and create brain-to-brain language connections. Mastering the movements involved in spoken (and written) language is thus another major childhood movement task.

Children who hope to drive a car at age 16 seem to know intuitively that they had better get on a tricycle at three, and similarly, to begin with video games at an early age if they hope to travel the Internet effectively by adolescence (the Internet being much like an almost infinite video game).

We're fascinated by those who move (or move objects) at virtuoso levels. The whole world gathers at the Olympic Games every two years to discover who can jump the highest, throw things the farthest, run or skate the fastest, ski the best. We attend concerts to observe others sing or play musical instruments and sporting events to watch others throw balls through hoops or hit them with bats. It may seem kind of foolish, but it's also quite human.

The sea squirt has a brain during its juvenile period. It swims about looking for a place that's rich in the nutrients it needs to survive. When it locates such a place, it backs into a cleft in a rock or coral and begins the rest of its now immobile life by eating its now superfluous brain. So it seems that when you've located a place to settle down and simply allow the resources you need to come to you, you don't really need a brain. You may have observed this phenomenon in universities when a professor gets tenure.

Although billions of neurons may be involved in a decision to move, only about a half million motor neurons are actually involved in activating the muscle groups that make up almost half of our body weight—the more than 650 skeletal muscles that connect pairs of bones, and the heart, intestines, tongue, and eye muscles that do other wondrous things. The visible parts of our brain's motor system are thus dependent on a complex underlying cognitive support system.

Think of an airline. The pilot of a commercial airliner is generally seen as the most important person in a flight. The pilot, however, gets paid principally for flying the first and last few minutes of the flight. The automatic pilot does much of the flying between takeoff and landing, while the pilot monitors the instruments. Furthermore, the flight itself depends on a large and less visible support staff who do the preliminary work of purchasing and maintaining the airplanes, planning routes and schedules, handling reservations and ticket sales, and maintaining airports.

Our motor system has an analogous three-part arrangement. Many sections of our brain, especially the frontal lobes, are involved in the thinking and planning processes that lead to a conscious decision to move, such as to walk to a nearby store. Our conscious starting, walking, and stopping actions are processed principally in the motor cortex and basal ganglia. Our cerebellum at the lower back of our brain (our brain's equivalent of an automatic pilot) takes over the routine repeated walking actions shortly after we consciously begin, and so most of our walk to the store becomes an automatic act. Our basal ganglia and other brain areas monitor the trip, and resume conscious control whenever conscious movements are required (such as to cross a busy street or to walk around an obstruction), much as when the plane pilot takes over from the automatic pilot when flight conditions warrant it.

This shifting back and forth between conscious and automatic movements is very useful in that it frees our conscious brain from routine actions so that we can converse with a friend, think, and enjoy the view during the walk—things we couldn't easily do if we had to consciously direct our feet with right-foot, left-foot, right-foot, left-foot commands during the walk. Or imagine if we had to consciously move our tongue and lips while we talked.

People with Parkinson's disease suffer from neuronal death in the basal ganglia area. Their brain can decide to walk, but they can't consciously initiate the appropriate movements. They can generally continue to walk if someone gets them started, but they can't consciously fine-tune their movements or stop when they want to. The brain areas that regulate planning activities and automatic movements function, but it's as if the pilot didn't show up to take off and land the planes in an otherwise functioning airline. See Figures 6 and 10.

See also Basal Ganglia, Cerebellum, Cognitive and Motor Degeneration, Motor Cortex, Peripheral Nervous System

Music

A form of communication in all cultures that uses such aural elements as tone, melody, harmony, rhythm, and volume to carry its emotionally loaded message.

Music may well have been the precursor to human language. Our innate ability to recognize and respond to rhythms and tonal variations may have eventually led to the greater communicative complexities of language. When we humans went beyond birdsong and primate vocal signals to develop language, we may have pre-served music because it provided human life and discourse with important supplementary emotional overtones.

Adjectives and adverbs expand the categorical information in nouns and verbs, and good storytellers can evoke powerful feelings through words alone. But songs exponentially expand the power of speech by inserting musical emotion into articulate communication.

Songs are typically cognitive commentaries on dangers and opportunities. Their basic message is quite simple—*I like* or *I dislike* something. In songs, we tend to like basic emotionally loaded things such as lovers, family, God, country, holidays, seasons, and sports teams, and we tend to dislike such things as war, unrequited love, unfaithful lovers, and bad times.

So if all George Frederick Handel wanted to say was, "Hallelujah, for the Lord God Omnipotent reigneth," why did it take him five minutes to say it? By extending vowel sounds and repeat-ing words and phrases, songs slow down the expression of the basic message to attach the emotional power of melody, harmony, rhythm, and volume. The performance of the "Hallelujah Chorus" thus exalts the relatively simple and straightforward message well beyond its textual expression—and many people who disagree with its religious message find themselves emotionally moved by its musical expres-sion. That's the power of music.

Music doesn't need words to communicate emotion. Symphony orchestras, jazz combos, and marching bands play dramatically different styles of music without lyrics, evoking a unique emotional response from each listener. Although every listener hears the same musical message, interpretations of it can differ significantly.

Music is obviously not a language in the same sense that English is a language, because sequences of notes or chords don't have the same precise meanings that sequences of letters and words do. Still, most of us tend to recognize certain tonal sequences and chords as music and consider other sequences to be mere noise, so music does have a culturally related sense of tonal sequence and grammar to it, albeit one different from that of the phoneme-and-letter sequences of any spoken or written language.

Still, we can think of music (and especially song) as a form of language. In articulate speech, we can communicate a lot of information in a relatively short period of time by compressing the message into a stream of rapidly flowing phonemic sounds that insert the meaning into the sound sequence rather than into the phonemes themselves (as in *do, dog, god, good, goods*). In song, conversely, we communicate a short but emotionally strong message of love and hate, of commitment and alienation, by slowing it down via the musical elements that add its emotional power.

And it is interesting, isn't it, that children spend much of the first 10 years of their life mastering the vocabulary and syntax of oral and written language and that adolescence in probably the one decade in our life during which we're most fascinated by music. It's the decade during which we develop our personal and social identity that music helps us to explore so well.

Music has an innate neurological base because all scaled forms of music are based on octaves, intervals, and harmonics, even though cultural differences and preferences do exist. Music has to function within the dimensions of human auditory capability.

For most people, music processing is centered in the right hemisphere (although rhythm is one element of music that's processed in the left hemisphere). Birds process their songs in the left hemisphere, where we typically process language. If music was a precursor to human language, it's possible that most of our brain's musical functions shifted over to the right hemisphere when the complexities of language began to dominate our left hemisphere functions. Trained musicians often activate left hemisphere processing systems while listening to music, probably because they're also analyzing the music. Most of us just turn on our right hemisphere and enjoy the music. See Figure 6.

See also Cerebral Hemispheres, Emotion and Feelings, Language

Myelin. *See* Neuron

N

Nature and Nurture

The issue of the relative levels of influence that genetic inheritance (nature) and life experience (nurture) play in determining our traits and capabilities.

Our some 30,000 genes are our parents' initial gift at conception—the book of instructions on how to construct and operate our body. It includes useful directions on such basic things as gender; body organization; skin, hair, and eye color; and temperament. About nine months later, our parents discover how their combined genetic directions turned out, and they're usually pleased. We all love our babies, who tend to (at least somewhat) resemble us.

Thirty thousand genes are enough to direct the embryo, fetus, and then the infant on how to develop and operate a basic birth body, but they're not enough to provide specific directions for living out our complex, extended life. So the nature-nurture issue revolves around the relative levels of influence that our genes and our life experiences have on who we become.

To simplify a complex biological system, a gene is the section of the long convoluted DNA molecule that prescribes the sequence of amino acids that make up a specific protein, and proteins define much of our physical self—we're kind of a big sack of proteins. Genetics thus would certainly influence such protein properties as height and body shape, but diet and exercise could alter such basic genetic plans.

The nature/nurture issue has political overtones. Folks who believe that nurture is the primary influence in a person's maturation and lifestyle strongly support social service and education programs, and especially those that help folks at the lower ends of various human attainment scales. They say in effect: Imagine a goal, strive toward it, and we'll help you to achieve it.

Folks who believe that nature is the primary influence in who we become are less inclined to support massive programs that hope to improve human conditions they feel can't be changed. They say in effect: Accept your abilities and limitations, and we'll do our best to create a broad accepting society that can accommodate a wide range of capabilities and personalities.

What scientists now understand is that neither extreme position is correct. Some human properties such as height and skin color are genetically determined and almost impossible to change, but other properties such as the language we speak and the cultural traditions we follow are almost entirely based on experience.

Scientists use a measure called heritability that statistically estimates how much nature and nurture contribute to the individual variation observable in a trait. For example, are differences in susceptibility to an illness more related to family lineage or to such environmental factors as diet, environmental pollutants, and so on? Scientists compare the total amount of variation in susceptibility within a population with the level of susceptibility within specific families. If relatively few people within the general population are susceptible to the illness, but those within certain family groups are much more susceptible, the illness would be considered heritable. Conversely, even though the chances of being injured in a logging accident are higher than in the general population if you are a member of a family of loggers, that susceptibility wouldn't be heritable. Fingerprint patterns are thus considered heritable, but calluses are occupational (or environmental).

If a trait is said to be 70% heritable, that doesn't mean that 70% of the trait is due to genetics and 30% to the environment. Rather, it suggests that 70% of the observed variation in that trait in a specific sample of people can be attributed to genetics and 30% to environmental factors.

Most people have difficulty understanding the subtle complexities of genetics, but we're all increasingly being drawn into moral and political controversies over genetics-related issues. Indeed, scientists have recently announced the successful cloning of a human embryo. This development will certainly exacerbate an already contentious discussion of the cultural appropriateness of such research. The resolution of such issues in our democratic society will involve many voters and politicians who unfortunately don't really understand the underlying science implicit in the decisions they'll make. It's the task of educators to see that the next generation is informed.

See also Deoxyribonucleic Acid (DNA), Plasticity

References

Marcus, G. (2004). *The birth of the mind: How a tiny number of genes creates the complexities of human thought.* New York: Basic Books.
Ridley, M. (2000). *Genome: The autobiography of a species in 23 chapters.* New York: Perennial.

Nerve

Bundles of neuronal axons in the peripheral nervous system that bring sensory information into the brain or that carry motor commands from the brain.

Bundles of axons within the brain are commonly called tracts.

See also Neuron, Peripheral Nervous System

Nervous System

A complex network of body and brain neurons that communicate sensorimotor information and thought processes.

The nervous system encompasses the central nervous system (brain and spinal cord) and the peripheral nervous system (sensorimotor neurons outside the brain and spinal cord). The peripheral nervous system's complementary sympathetic and parasympathetic subsystems process unconscious autonomic (automatic) functions.

The sympathetic system unconsciously activates fight/flight responses during imminent danger or opportunity, and the parasympathetic system slows down body alertness functions during other times to rest and recuperate.

See also Central Nervous System, Nerve, Neuron, Peripheral Nervous System

Neurology. *See* Brain Sciences

Neuron (NUR-on)

A specialized cell within an information network that includes our brain, sense organs, muscles, and glands. A neuron exchanges molecular information with other specific cells via multiple sending and receiving extensions from its cell body. Most neuronal communication is within brain networks rather than between brain and body.

Humans have an estimated 100 billion neurons organized into complex networks. An average human head has 10,000 hairs, so humans have as many neurons as the amount of hair in a population of 10 million people (such as metropolitan New York City). A neuron can directly interact with thousands of other cells, so the molecular information in a neuron is only a few neurons away from any other neuron. If you think this is implausible, consider the 1 billion telephones in the world and the relatively simple coding system of up to a dozen digits that can rapidly connect any two phones.

Although all neurons have a characteristic organization, they do exhibit structural differences that enhance their various functions. The entries on the cerebellum and cerebral cortex will identify some of the most important types.

Neurons are beautifully organized to carry out their functions. Think of the human arm as a simple model of the neuron's three functional parts: The fingers represent the neuron's multiple dendrites that receive touch information; the hand represents the neuron's cell body that processes the information; and the arm represents the (normally single) axon that transmits touch information along the information chain to our brain.

A neuron's cell body contains all the structures that maintain cellular functions. An individual neuron can remain functional throughout our lifetime, but it rebuilds itself every three months or so, molecule by molecule as parts wear out. The cell body and its DNA genetic system use the nutrients from the circulatory system to maintain the cell and to synthesize the neurotransmitter molecules that are central to its communications with other cells.

A neuron may interact with thousands of other cells, some of them quite far away (in cellular terms). The cell body thus contains separate sets of tubular sending (axon) and receiving (dendrite) extensions that keep the neurotransmitter molecules and their information within the extended cell body as they are transported to specific cells elsewhere in the neuronal network.

The typical neuron contains many short, fingerlike tubular extensions called dendrites that receive information from other neurons. Dendrites can extend a millimeter or so into the surrounding area, which doesn't seem like much until you realize how densely packed neurons are. Dendrites contain many receptors—protein molecules that extend through the dendrite's membrane to receive chemical messages carried by another neuron's neurotransmitter molecules. Spines may develop on dendrites during memory formation, increasing the number of receptors and therefore the amount of neurotransmitter information that can enter the neuron at one time.

A typical neuron has an axon extension that sends the neuron's message to other neurons in the circuit. Motor neuron axons that extend from brain to muscles can be a meter or more in length, but most axons are in the millimeter range. The axon may divide into branches toward its end and thus send its message to many other cells. The ending of an axon is called a terminal or bouton, and it is here that a neuron stores its neurotransmitters in little packets called vesicles while they wait to be released.

Neuronal Transmission. Neuron cells bodies and their many dendrite extensions constantly receive various levels of excitatory (send) and inhibitory (don't send) information from related neurons. This information is averaged within the cell body, and if it reaches the neuron's firing threshold (send) at a given moment, an action potential develops, and the message rapidly moves along the axon to the terminal in a process called depolarization. This movement of a neural message along an axon has been likened to an electrical charge. It does have some similarities, but neural messages don't move in the same way that electrical currents do. It is also more complicated biochemically than the following, but you should be able to use this brief functional explanation with students:

The inside of an axon has a slight negative charge, and the fluids outside the axon have a slight positive charge. When a neuron reaches its firing threshold, it propagates a signal down the axon that rapidly opens and closes a series of channels (pores in the axon membrane through which electrically charged ions can pass). When a set of depolarized channels opens, positively charged sodium ions from the fluids outside the neuron enter the axon. This action briefly changes the charge inside that part of the axon from negative to positive, and this also triggers the opening of the next set of channels. The process is then repeated with the next set of channels. Think of a row of dominoes falling over. Each domino pushes the next one, just as each set of channels opens the next set.

After a set of channels opens, the sodium ions are pumped out, the channels close, and that part of the axon once again has a negative charge, until the next axon potential propagates down the axon.

One type of glial cell (oligodendrocytes) wraps itself around long axons, creating a kind of intermittent insulating layer called myelin. This wrapping process reduces the number of functioning sodium channels along the axon, and thus speeds up the message. The places in myelinated axons where channels remain open are called nodes of Ranvier. Think of an unmyelinated axon as a slow local train (5 miles per hour) that stops at every station, and a myelinated axon as a fast express train (200 miles per hour) that stops infrequently.

When the axon's wave of permeability to sodium ions (the sequential opening and closing of channels) reaches the axon terminal, calcium ions enter the terminal, triggering the release of packets (vesicles) of neurotransmitters into the synapse, a very narrow gap between the axon of one neuron and the dendrite of another. The neurotransmitters attach to the appropriate receptors in the dendrites or cell body of the postsynaptic neuron, and thereby pass their neuron's molecular message on to the next neuron. Most neurotransmitters then return to the terminal via reuptake channels for reuse in subsequent action potentials. See Figures 1 and 2.

See also Cell, Cerebellum, Cerebral Cortex, Glia, Interneuron, Membrane, Mirror Neurons, Neurotransmitter, Nucleus, Postsynaptic Neuron, Presynaptic Neuron, Receptor

Neuroscience. *See* Brain Sciences

Neurosis

A somewhat nebulous concept that encompasses relatively mild but maladaptive anxious behaviors that seemingly have no organic cause.

Neurotic behavior seems removed from reality with its continuing anxiety about something that doesn't bother most people, such as a fear of heights or crowds or a compulsion for cleanliness or order. Neurosis can be contrasted with psychosis, which is far more maladaptive and has an organic base.

See also Psychosis

Neurotransmitter

A molecule that plays a key role in the movement of information within the nervous system. It is released from a presynaptic neuron and diffuses across the narrow synaptic gap to attach to a receptor on the postsynaptic neuron, thus moving molecular information from one neuron to another.

The information that neurons process is coded into chemical molecules called neurotransmitters and into their distribution patterns. Molecules are formed from two or more atoms. In our brain, the principal atoms are carbon, oxygen, nitrogen, and hydrogen. Between 10 and 30 atoms join to form each of the 20 types of amino acids that are the building blocks of our brain's protein, hormone, and neurotransmitter molecules.

The amino acids that make up a protein molecule are assembled in a linear sequence within a cell (following genetic directions coded into DNA in the cell's nucleus), and this chain then twists itself into a characteristic globular shape before leaving the cell to carry out its intended protein functions. The whole process takes a few minutes. The pattern of electronic properties that arises out of a molecule's shape determines the effect it will have on cells and other molecules.

Scientists have identified more than 50 neurotransmitters and will probably identify more before the entire system is understood. Neurotransmitters stimulate, inhibit, or modulate the actions of the neurons to which they attach. Neurotransmitters carry out their various communicative functions at the synapse, a narrow gap between the axon terminal of a presynaptic neuron and (principally) the dendrites of a postsynaptic neuron. The postsynaptic dendrites contain receptors—protein molecules that project through the dendrite's membrane.

Although the process is a bit more complicated than the following analogy, think of a receptor as a lock and a neurotransmitter as a key. The shape of the neurotransmitter (key) interacts with the shape of the receptor (lock). If it's a good match, the neurotransmitter transmits its message to the postsynaptic neuron. Like a key that's returned to one's pocket after opening the door, many neurotransmitters are pumped back into the presynaptic terminal after release from the receptor and used again.

Synapses are busy places with a multitude of neurotransmitters. If the number and intensity of the various molecular messages simultaneously entering a postsynaptic neuron reach the postsynaptic neuron's firing threshold (think of a thermostat), the chemical message translates into an impulse that travels along the axon. When the impulse reaches the presynaptic axon terminal, it releases neurotransmitters into the synapse, where they cross to the postsynaptic dendrites, and the communication process thus continues from neuron to neuron.

Our brain's dozens of types of neurotransmitters can be classified both functionally and chemically.

Functional Classification. A neurotransmitter sends either an excitatory or inhibitory message to the receiving neuron. An excitatory message helps to increase the subsequent communicative actions of the postsynaptic neuron, and an inhibitory message helps to reduce them. Think of an off/on switch or the binary number system. The chemical composition of the neurotransmitter interacting with its target receptor determines the nature and complexity of the message.

Why do our brain's neurons need dozens of different types of neurotransmitters to communicate two basic verblike messages: *send* or *don't send*? Perhaps for the same reason that our language has dozens of verbs to express the basic message *Move your body by moving your legs,* when the verb *walk* expresses the basic idea. Words such as *run, dance, hop, jog,* and *skip* add information to the basic concept. Think also of the modulating effects of adverbs on verbs, and adjectives on nouns. Similarly, the variety and complexity of excitatory and inhibitory neurotransmitters probably add some form of currently ill-understood supplementary information to the basic molecular message.

Neural activity in our brain is fortunately much more inhibitory than excitatory. At any given moment, we focus our attention, limit our activity, and ignore most of our memories. Imagine life with a principally excitatory brain that continually attended to everything, carried out all possible actions, and had continual access to all prior experiences!

Chemical Classification. Almost all of our brain's 50-plus types of neurotransmitters can be chemically classified into three categories:

- *Amino Acids.* Four chemically simple amino acids form one class of neurotransmitters. Glutamate and aspartate are excitatory neurotransmitters. GABA (gamma-amniobutyric acid) and glycine are inhibitory neurotransmitters. Glutamate and GABA are the principal verblike neurotransmitters in the cerebral cortex (*send, don't send*). Glycine is a major neurotransmitter in the brainstem and spinal cord.

- *Monoamines.* The six types of monoamine neurotransmitters are acetylcholine, dopamine, histamine, norepinephrine (or noradrenalin), epinephrine, and serotonin. They are chemically modified amino acids that act more slowly than the amino acid neurotransmitters. Each type is synthesized in a single brainstem or limbic system source, and its circuitry spreads widely from there throughout the brain (think of a small lawn sprinkler that distributes water to a large lawn area). The monoamines modulate the actions of the amino acid neurotransmitters (think of the modulating actions of adverbs on verbs). The interaction of a monoamine neurotransmitter with its postsynaptic receptor helps to determine the nature of the message. The six monoamine neurotransmitters are discussed in more detail under their own entries in this book.

- *Peptides.* The largest and most complex neurotransmitters are the peptides (or neuropeptides), such as oxytocin and endorphin. They are composed of chains of 2 to 39 amino acids. Most of the dozens of types of neurotransmitters in our brain and peripheral nervous system are peptides, but their concentrations are much lower than that of the amino acids and monoamines (which are also known as the *classical neurotransmitters*). Many neurons that distribute a classical neurotransmitter also distribute a peptide that increases or decreases the postsynaptic neuron's receptivity of the neuron's primary transmitter, thus modulating its effect.

Peptides use neural networks, our circulatory system, and air passages to travel throughout our body and brain to modulate the broad range of pleasure and pain. A peptide action that occurs simultaneously in a large number of related cells can powerfully affect the decisions we make within the continuum of emotionally charged approaching and retreating behaviors, such as to drink/urinate, agree/disagree, buy/sell, and marry/divorce. In effect, the shifts in the body and brain levels of these molecules allocate our emotional energy: what to do, when to do it, and how much energy to expend on the activity.

A peptide's message can vary in different body and brain areas, just as a two-by-four can be used in many ways in the construction of a house. For example, angiotensin is a peptide that activates the seeking and conserving behaviors that regulate our body's fluid levels. In our brain, it does this principally by activating feelings of thirst and the consequent behaviors that seek water. In our body, it causes kidneys to conserve water. The situation is similar with many drugs. For example, alcohol can excite or sedate, depending on the amount ingested and the drinker's emotional state. Endorphins can similarly reduce intense pain and increase euphoria.

The following more commonly known peptides are discussed in their own entries in this book: angiotensin II, cholecystokinin, endorphin (enkephalin, dynorphin), oxytocin, somatostatin, substance P, and vasopressin. See Figures 1 and 2.

See also Cell, Drugs, Neuron. The neurotransmitters listed here are also listed as entries.

Nodes of Ranvier

The small regions of bare axons on otherwise myelinated neurons. Channels for sodium-potassium exchange exist only at these gaps (rather than all along the axon), and so the action potential jumps from node to node and this speeds up the transmission time from cell body to axon terminal. See Figure 1.

See also Neuron

Norepinephrine (NOR-epee-nef-rin)

The primary neurotransmitter in the sympathetic nervous system for regulating blood pressure and activating stress-related fight/flight responses. It's also called noradrenaline.

Norepinephrine is synthesized in both the brainstem's locus ceruleus (from which it spreads throughout the brain as a regulatory mechanism) and the adrenal glands. Epinephrine (or adrenaline) is chemically and functionally related to norepinephrine and dopamine (collectively known as the catecholamines). See Figures 5 and 7.

See also Brainstem, Epinephrine, Neurotransmitter, Peripheral Nervous System

Nucleus

A somewhat confusing term, because it refers to two separate concepts in biology: (1) A cell nucleus contains the cell's tightly packed genetic material—the long, twisted DNA molecule that provides the genetic directions for protein synthesis and that splits during cell division (mitosis). (2) A brain nucleus is a relatively small cluster of related neurons that carry out a specific brain task. For example, the nucleus accumbens is considered our brain's pleasure center, with many connections to other areas that process emotion. An analogous related cluster of neurons in the peripheral nervous system is called a ganglion.

A cell nucleus thus regulates cellular activity and a brain nucleus regulates a specific brain activity. See Figure 1.

See also Basal Ganglia, Cell, Deoxyribonucleic Acid (DNA), Nucleus Accumbens

Nucleus Accumbens

A basal ganglia structure within the dopamine circuitry that is associated with pleasure and reward and strongly implicated in addiction.

See also Basal Ganglia, Dopamine, Drugs, Ganglion

Nurture. *See* Nature and Nurture

Nutrition

The kind, quality, and quantity of the food we ingest to stay healthy and alive.

The brain is made up of the same materials as the body, so its nutrient needs are similar. Glucose is central to neuronal processing, and amino acids to neurotransmitter synthesis. Blood that is rich in oxygen and nutrients leaves the heart via the aorta, flows into the head via the carotid artery, and then travels throughout the body. Our brain is thus first in line for nutritional support—and it certainly fills its plate. Although our brain encompasses only 2% of our body's weight, it uses 20% of all our nutrient energy. When we're especially active, our brain uses almost as much oxygen as all our muscles combined.

The blood-brain barrier is a protective layer surrounding our brain's blood vessels (and especially capillaries). It allows useful materials to pass from the circulatory system into brain tissue but prevents most potentially dangerous materials from entering into brain tissue.

A reasonably wholesome, balanced diet will take care of our brain's nutrient needs, although the rest of our body (which gets the leavings) may not do as well. The dilemma is to know for sure what a wholesome balanced diet is, given the variety of current perspectives on nutrition (and that issue is beyond the scope of this book). Even with all the dietary disagreement, children with a developing brain and body should avoid what are commonly called junk foods and carbonated beverages and explore the wide range of foods commonly known to be wholesome.

See also Amino Acid, Blood-Brain Barrier, Glucose

O

Obsessive-Compulsive Disorder

An anxiety disorder characterized by distressing, obsessive thoughts or fears and by compulsions to perform one or more ritualistic behaviors (such as washing one's hands, counting things repeatedly, or hoarding useless objects), often to alleviate the obsession. The afflicted person knows that the obsessive thoughts don't really make sense and that his or her compulsive behaviors are counterproductive and provide no feelings of satisfaction.

Obsessive-compulsive disorder (OCD) affects about 3% of the population, with an onset in adolescence or early adult life, and no marked gender preference. OCD is principally a frontal lobe disorder in that our brain's decision-making systems seem locked into a behavior like a car stuck in a gear, unable to go on. Successful medical and behavioral interventions have recently emerged.

See also Tourette's Syndrome

Occipital Lobes

Paired sensory lobes in the upper back section of the cerebral cortex that participate in the recognition of dangers and opportunities, focusing especially on the various elements of vision (shape, depth, color, movement).

Imagine an ear-to-ear line across your skull. The occipital, temporal, and parietal sensory lobes of the cerebral cortex are located principally in the back (above the thalamus), and the frontal lobes are in the front (above the basal ganglia). The occipital lobes are located behind the temporal and parietal lobes.

The back-to-front organizing principle of both the cortical and subcortical areas is that the brain's back section recognizes and creates mental models of dangers and opportunities, and the front section manipulates and transforms these models into a response that it then initiates. Although the occipital lobes are the smallest of the four sets of lobes (18% of the cerebral cortex), the visual system plays a central role in human sensory processing. See Figures 6 and 8.

See also Basal Ganglia, Cerebral Cortex, Cerebral Hemispheres, Cerebrum, Frontal Lobes, Occipital Lobes, Parietal Lobes, Sight, Thalamus

Olfactory Bulb. *See* Smell

Oligodendrocyte. *See* Glia

Operant Conditioning. *See* Conditioning

Oxytocin (ox-e-TOSE-in)

A pituitary peptide that initiates the uterine contractions and lactation in childbirth and breast-feeding. Oxytocin and another pituitary peptide called vasopressin play key roles in enhancing social and bonding behaviors, especially between sexual partners and between parents and children. Oxytocin levels tend to be higher in females and vasopressin levels tend to be higher in males.

See also Neuron, Neurotransmitter, Pituitary Gland, Vasopressin

P

Parallel Processing

An important cognitive property in which multiple elements of a phenomenon or multiple phenomena are processed simultaneously in various brain areas.

We have a modular brain with hundreds of separate systems (or modules) that are specialized to process the sensory, problem-solving, and motor activities that characterize a behavior. For example, separate brain areas process color, shape, quantity, and movement, so these areas would be simultaneously active while a person observes a single red ball rolling across a table.

Computers typically use a serial processing system in which data are rapidly but individually processed in a fixed logical sequence. Serial systems are fast and precise; parallel systems are slower but more adaptable to error. A computer is a remarkable computational device, but it's unable to proceed if a letter is omitted in an e-mail address—something a brain would typically spot and correct.

Paranoia

A delusional psychotic disorder in which afflicted people incorrectly believe that they are being unfairly persecuted or that they have achieved superior celebrity status (delusions of grandeur).

See also Psychosis

Parasympathetic Nervous System.
See Peripheral Nervous System

Parietal Lobes

Paired sensory lobes in the upper back section of the cerebral cortex that participate in the recognition of dangers and opportunities, focusing especially on touch sensations, body and joint orientation, and space-location relationships.

Imagine an ear-to-ear line across your skull. The occipital, temporal, and parietal sensory lobes of the cerebral cortex are principally located in the back (above the thalamus), and the frontal lobes are in the front (above the basal ganglia). The parietal lobes (encompassing 19% of the cerebral cortex) are located between the occipital and frontal lobes and above the temporal lobes.

The back-to-front organizing principle of both the cortical and subcortical areas is that the brain's back section recognizes and creates mental models of dangers and opportunities, and the front section manipulates and transforms these models into a response that it then initiates. See Figure 6.

See also Basal Ganglia, Cerebral Cortex, Cerebral Hemispheres, Cerebrum, Frontal Lobes, Occipital Lobes, Temporal Lobes, Thalamus, Touch

Parkinson's Disease.
See Cognitive and Motor Degeneration

Parvocellular. *See* Sight

Peptide. *See* Neurotransmitter

Perception

The subjective interpretation of incoming sensory information.

Our sense organs feed a continuous flow of external and internal environmental information into the posterior regions of the sensory lobes of the cerebral cortex. This information is then sent forward into sensory lobe areas that consciously and unconsciously integrate it into a perceptual or interpretive map of the current external-internal environment—in effect, the cause, source, and personal meaning of the sensory information. Our brain often must quickly and accurately perceive in order to respond effectively to the immediate challenge. A series of rapid, related perceptions can lead to the development of a useful generalized remembered concept that then enhances subsequent related perceptual processing and problem solving.

See also Sensory System

Peripheral Nervous System

All elements of the nervous system that aren't within the brain and spinal cord (the central nervous system). These include (1) the 12 pairs of cranial nerves that help process facial sensorimotor activity and some autonomic glandular and organ functions, and (2) the 31 pairs of spinal nerves that move sensory information from body regions to the spinal cord and move motor information from the spinal cord to muscles.

The complementary sympathetic and parasympathetic subsystems process unconscious autonomic (automatic) functions of the peripheral nervous system. The sympathetic system unconsciously activates during imminent danger or opportunity. A stress (or fight/flight) response basically increases blood flow to the large muscles and decreases body activities (such as digestion) that take energy away from what is needed for a quick vigorous response. Conversely, the parasympathetic system slows down body alertness functions to rest and recuperate (and resume digestion). Think of the sympathetic system as a gas pedal and the parasympathetic system as a brake. You can't activate them simultaneously, but both play important functions along the road of life.

See also Central Nervous System, Meninges, Stress

PET (Positron Emission Tomography).
See Brain Imaging Technology

Pheromone (FEAR-oh-moan)

A class of powerful, hormone-like molecules that animals pass on to others within their species through the air or physical contact to communicate specific sexual or social messages.

A female moth emitting a minute quantity of pheromones can draw a male moth to her from miles away. Pheromones enter the tiny vomeronasal organ in the human nose, but they are not part of our sense of smell. Rather, we might consider them a currently ill-understood sixth sense. They trigger neural activity in areas of the amygdala and hypothalamus that regulate sexual behavior and levels of comfort and self-confidence. Pheromones have been tentatively associated with the human allure of certain perfumes, the attraction of truffles (and their relationship to underarm sweat), and the tendency of women who live together to develop synchronized menstrual cycles.

The cheek area next to our nose contains many pheromones, and this may explain why we humans like to kiss by nuzzling our nose into that pheromone-rich area. Although the effect of pheromones on human behavior is still something of a mystery, one can muse on their possible effects on hundreds of adolescent students bound together for hours in an enclosed school environment.

See also Smell

Phoneme

The fundamental sound unit of speech.

All words are composed of sequences of meaningless (vowel and consonant) phonemes that gain meaning through their sequence and the length of the phonemic chain (*do, dog, god, good, goods*). The number and set of phonemes will differ in various languages, but all phonemes must function within human vocal and auditory capabilities. Most languages have about four dozen phonemes, but the range encompasses the Maori language with 15 phonemes to English with 44 to the African Khoisan language with 141 (including click sounds unique to northern African languages). Infants can respond to all human language phonemes until the phonemes of their native language dominate their language experience, after which their ability to recognize nonnative phonemes diminishes.

See also Aphasia, Language, Mirror Neurons

Pia Mater. *See* Meninges

Pineal Gland (PINE-nee-el)

A small neuroendocrine gland that produces the melatonin that helps to regulate sleeping/waking states. The pineal gland is located just under the back end of the corpus callosum. Most brain structures are doubled, but the pineal gland is a single structure. See Figure 7.

See also Corpus Callosum, Melatonin, Sleep

Pituitary Gland (pih-TOO-i-tairy)

The pea-sized, garlic-bulb-shaped master gland of the endocrine system (although it's located in the brain, below the hypothalamus).

The pituitary gland produces a large number of hormones that affect the activity of every endocrine gland and body activity—such as bone and muscle growth, circulation and water balance, the secretion of testosterone and estrogen, ovulation, and uterine contractions. The pituitary gland activates the adrenal gland to initiate a stress response. See Figure 7.

See also Endocrine Glands, Hypothalamus, Stress

Planum Temporale (PLAY-num tempo-RAL-e)

A temporal lobe region that encompasses Wernicke's area. It is associated with language comprehension and in most people is considerably larger in the hemisphere that is dominant for language (typically the left hemisphere). See Figure 6.

See also Temporal Lobes, Wernicke's Area

Plasticity

The critically important capability of our brain's neurons and processing systems to change in structure, function, or both in response to new challenges.

Although many of our 30,000 genes are dedicated to developing our brain, human life is so complex and changeable that genetics alone can't possibly prepare us for every challenge we might confront. What our genes thus provide at birth is a one-pound basic but adaptable human brain that needs parental support. Our brain expands to its three-pound autonomous adult size because its plasticity allows growth, development, and learning to occur. Learning is a lifelong process because of the dynamic plastic nature of neuronal networks. Some processing systems have innate developmental periods (such as the onset of walking at one year, speech at two years), and other processing systems depend on specific experiences and practice that some but not all children have (such as the ability to hit a baseball, to bake a cake).

How our brain's plasticity is triggered and executed is still not completely understood, but plasticity is apparently centered in changes that occur at the synapse where axons and dendrites interact through neurotransmitter exchange—and so establish and alter neuronal networks. It's not surprising that younger brains are more plastic than older brains. Young, inexperienced brains still have many interconnection options. Processing systems in mature brains become more established as experience shapes an efficient brain tuned to the typical challenges we confront. A young brain can thus lose an entire hemisphere and transfer its functions into the surviving hemisphere. An old brain suffering a stroke in a small hemispheric area may never recover the function. Recent advances in rehabilitation optimistically suggest that many disabilities that were formerly thought to be hopeless can now be alleviated through the emerging better understanding of brain plasticity.

Use analogies such as the following to explain how a mature brain can continually change and yet maintain its same three-pound size: I have about the same *number* of friends I had 10 years ago, but they're not necessarily the same people; I shop at the same *number* of stores I shopped at 10 years ago, but not necessarily the same stores. When we move, our brain must erase our old phone number and address and insert the new ones. I wear the same amount of clothing each day, but not the same articles of clothing.

See also Growth and Development, Neuron

Play and Games

Play: informal individual or small-group explorations with a minimal focus on a clearly defined goal. *Games:* the more organized and typically scored comparisons of specific skills exhibited by competing individuals or teams who have the same clearly defined goal.

An extended sheltered human maturation permits our early, gradual and informal exploration of the wide variety of survival problems and solutions that independent life will later present. When such learning occurs outside of school, it generally emerges through *play* and *games* and involves informal assessment. Conversely, school learning generally emerges through coerced *work* and involves a formal assessment. School is the only place in our society where learning is called work.

Our young will joyfully spend much personal time and energy on play and games that challenge them to master developmentally important knowledge and skills that connect novelty and familiarity to a problem that intrigues them. In this, they frequently have no conscious awareness of the developmental needs implicit in the activity. For example, children's universal fascination with scary stories, play, and games is probably related to their innate need to develop the brain systems that can properly process the important emotion of fear and to develop such systems in nonthreatening settings.

Our primary emotions are fear, anger, disgust, surprise, sadness, and joy, and we can add many secondary and blended emotions to that list (such as anticipation, tension, and pride). All involve the emotionally important cognitive arousal systems that must be developed and maintained for our brain to recognize dangers and opportunities. It's a use-it-or-lose-it proposition.

Some of these emotions may not be sufficiently activated in normal life. Play and games frequently and artificially activate fear (and its handmaiden, attention), however, and this may partly explain our culture's strong and enduring interest in play and games. Note how all the other emotions (and attention) play similarly key roles in play and games.

The arts play related integrative roles in the development and maintenance of many of our brain's processing systems. Arts experiences that interest us tend to relate to important personal concerns. They thus allow us to explore the topics in a nonthreatening playlike manner during periods when we're not actually confronted by the problem in its real form, and so they help us to develop and maintain the emotion, attention, and problem-solving systems that normally process the challenge.

The recent reductions in school arts programs and an atmosphere of play are thus a biological tragedy that we'll come to regret when our society matures in its understanding of our brain's developmental and maintenance needs.

Pons. *See* Hindbrain

Postsynaptic Neuron

The neuron in a synaptic cleft that contains receptors capable of receiving (binding) neurotransmitters released into the synapse by a presynaptic neuron. See Figures 1 and 2.

See also Neuron, Presynaptic Neuron, Synapse

Prefrontal Cortex. *See* Frontal Lobes

Presynaptic Neuron

The neuron in a synaptic cleft that releases neurotransmitters from its axon terminal into the synapse. These neurotransmitters will cross the synaptic gap and bind with receptors on the postsynaptic neuron. See Figures 1 and 2.

See also Neuron, Postsynaptic Neuron, Synapse

Problem Solving

Cognitive strategies used to define challenges and search for effective and appropriate solutions.

We have two separate solution and response systems: (1) Challenges with a sense of immediacy are rapidly and reflexively processed by our brain's innate stress-driven, conceptual (principally subcortical) problem-solving system. This system responds quickly on the basis of the small amount of emotionally intense information that's typically available. It's thus quite vulnerable to making impetuous, racist, sexist, or elitist responses that focus on only a few highly visible emotion-charged elements. (2) Challenges without a sense of immediacy are processed more slowly and reflectively by our brain's curiosity-driven, analytical (principally cortical) problem-solving system.

We thus will respond *reflexively* to a car moving swiftly toward us (conceptually concerned only with its looming rapid approach), but we'll generally respond *reflectively* to a car on a dealer's lot, if we're considering its purchase (and are thus concerned with its service history, possible malfunctioning systems, cost, etc.).

Our rapid reflexive system is the default system because it responds to dangers and opportunities that require an immediate decisive (fight/flight) response that will enhance survival. When it isn't immediately obvious whether a reflexive or reflective response is the more appropriate, both systems simultaneously search for a solution, with the reflexive system typically responding first.

Most of us thus ad hoc our way through life with a long string of regrets and apologies because of the late arrival of our brain's (often better) reflective response. Because many problems that humans now face don't require an impulsively reflexive response, the educational challenge is to help students develop and use their frontal lobe reflective capabilities in a low-threat environment. Such simulated experiences stored as memory can then be used later when students confront related real-life problems.

See also Emotion and Feelings, Growth and Development, Play and Games

Procedural Memory. *See* Memory

Psychiatry. *See* Brain Sciences

Psychosis

A serious brain disorder that leads to delusional or hallucinatory (or both) perceptions and thoughts.

Where neurosis is a relatively mild disassociation from reality, psychosis is so severe that it's difficult for the afflicted person to function effectively in a normal social environment without medical treatment. Schizophrenia is the most common form of psychosis.

See also Neurosis, Paranoia

Puberty and Adolescence

Puberty signals the onset of adolescence, and it's characterized principally by the emergence of sex hormones and secondary sexual characteristics.

We all meander into adult life through an adolescent door. Some go through it relatively easily, but most stumble as they cross the threshold—the erratic (and alas, often erotic) stumbling being almost a rite of passage. What's odd is that we adults so often seem surprised and even mystified when we observe adolescents confronting the same problems and doing the same foolish and destructive things that we did during our own passage. We often romanticize our own adolescence because we survived it, but now worry (as our parents worried about us) that our children won't survive.

The good news is that most adolescents finally make it through the door into responsible adulthood, and we now better understand the underlying biology that drives the maturation process—even though we still often don't know what to do about it.

Although puberty and adolescence are complex body/brain developmental phenomena, it's useful to think of adolescence as something that's especially focused in our brain's frontal lobes, where we process conscious executive decisions about what to do and how to do it. Considering that frontal lobe researchers metaphorically compare the role and importance of our frontal lobes to a corporation's CEO or to a symphony conductor, adolescent frontal lobe maturation is something to be praised and not ridiculed as it fine-tunes itself into adult competence.

The cultural strategy for dealing with children with immature frontal lobes is to expect the adults in their lives to make many frontal lobe decisions for them—where to live, what to wear, when to go to bed, and so forth. Children with immature frontal lobes are willing to let adults make such decisions. Infants who can't walk are similarly willing to let adults carry them. But just as young children generally don't want to be carried while they're learning to walk, adolescents don't want adults to make frontal lobe decisions for them while their frontal lobes are maturing.

The only way we can learn to walk is to practice walking, and the only way we can mature our frontal lobes is to practice the reflective problem-solving and advanced social skills that our frontal lobes process, even though young people initially aren't very successful with it. Adolescence thus becomes a challenge, both for adolescents and for the significant adults in their life.

Here's the problem: If a toddler falls down, the damage is usually minor. But an adolescent's awkwardness or bad decision can lead to something far more serious—an auto accident, a pregnancy.

As the potential for damage increases, the concern of the adults in an adolescent's life also increases.

Other developmental concerns: The adolescent brain is very sensitive to pleasure and reward, but their impulse control systems aren't yet mature. Adolescents are thus vulnerable to exploration with highly rewarding drugs—and alcohol and drugs negatively affect an adolescent brain much more than an adult brain.

Waking/sleeping habits change—adolescents seem to move two times zones west of where they live. Emotion, eating, motivation, and friendships follow a roller-coaster trajectory. It sometimes seems developmentally hopeless, but it isn't.

For example, the importance of extracurricular activities in a typical adolescent's school experience is centered on the many opportunities they provide for the development of autonomous decision making in a relatively safe and nonthreatening setting, with limited adult interference. Adolescence is also often a period of initial job experiences and the consequent need to relate to adults who aren't parents or teachers. Furthermore, adolescents are typically allowed to socialize with friends without parental supervision (albeit often with cell phone checkups). All these activities are developmentally important.

The adolescent years signal an appropriate temporary weakening of family bonds, as adolescents explore their need to adapt their family's rituals and traditions to those of nonkin peers with whom they will spend their adult life. Adolescents who are too tightly bound to their family won't be able to negotiate necessary compromises with potential mates and colleagues.

The middle school years, ages 11 to 15, that typically begin one's adolescence are somewhat analogous to the birth to age 4 preschool years. Both periods are characterized by initially slow and awkward capability with developmentally important tasks. The preschool years focus on sensory lobe problem recognition skills, and the middle school years focus on frontal lobe problem-solving skills. We're more accepting of the ineffectiveness of preschool children than we are of middle school children, but emerging middle school adolescents need the same kind of love and support that preschool children get—plus a gentle push toward the beginnings of autonomy. See Figure 6.

See also Frontal Lobes, Growth and Development, Hormones, Problem Solving

Reference

Strauch, B. (2003). *The primal teen: What the new discoveries about the teenage brain tell us about our kids.* New York: Doubleday.

Pulvinar

An important processing and relay element of the visual attention system, located at the back of the thalamus. See Figure 8.

See also Attention, Thalamus

Purkinje Cell. *See* Cerebellum

Pyramidal Cell. *See* Neuron

Q

Qualia

A philosophical term that refers to the qualitative aspects of a phenomenon (as differentiated from the quantitative or measurable aspects).

Qualia refer to common subjective experiences that are almost impossible to describe—the taste of coffee, the blueness of the sky, the feel of a caress, the smell of cinnamon, the sound of a church bell. It's impossible to feel the toothache another person is having even though we all have had toothaches, but it's easy to understand the quantitative aspects—that is, which tooth aches.

Within our brain, qualia represent the neuronal summary of the vast amount of information our brain has on an important element of the environment that's needed to understand and respond to a current challenge.

See also Consciousness

R

Raphe Nuclei (RAH-fey)

A group of brainstem nuclei involved in the synthesis of serotonin and the onset of sleep. See Figures 5 and 7.

See also Brainstem, Midbrain, Serotonin, Sleep

Receptor

Protein molecules that extend through a membrane (such as on a neuronal dendrite) to receive molecular messages (such as those carried by another neuron's neurotransmitter molecules).

See also Neuron

Reflex

An immediate predictable automatic response to a stimulus, often effected without any conscious awareness of the stimulus (such as an eye-blink response to a small approaching insect).

See also Stimulus

REM (Rapid Eye Movement). *See* Sleep

Reticular Formation

A netlike system of neurons in the central core of the brainstem that plays an important role in regulating and modulating survival functions and consciousness.

Reticular means "netlike," and that's a good way to think of the system—as a neural net that opens and closes to increase or decrease the amount of information that flows into and out of our brain. The reticular activating system is a key regulatory component in our level of alertness—from fully awake to sound asleep. See Figures 5 and 7.

See also Brainstem, Hindbrain, Locus Ceruleus, Midbrain, Pineal Gland, Raphe Nuclei, Sleep

Retina

A three-layer cellular sheet at the back of the eyeball that senses reflected light and initiates vision, turning the light that enters the eye into neuronal impulses that follow pathways that eventually reach the visual cortex and then other areas in the back of our brain where transmitted information about form, texture, color, depth, and movement becomes a perceptual map of the environment.

See also Sensory System, Sight

Retrograde Amnesia. *See* Amnesia

Rod. *See* Sight

S

Satellite Cells. *See* Glia

Schizophrenia (skits-o-FREE-nee-ah)

A debilitating mental illness (or perhaps a complex of several overlapping illnesses) that affects about 1% of the population, with onset typically occurring in late adolescence or early adulthood.

The term *schizophrenia* means "fragmented mind." Symptoms can be active (such as agitated, delusional, and hallucinatory behavior) or passive (such as disinterest in others and one's surroundings, emotional withdrawal, and irrational thought associations and speech).

The prevailing theory has been that schizophrenia is caused by excessive dopamine release in the limbic system and frontal lobes. Recent developments suggest, however, that other brain systems and neurotransmitters are also involved. Scientists are especially focusing on reduced levels of glutamate, an excitatory neurotransmitter that operates throughout our brain and so can affect the interactions among many systems necessary for efficient cognition.

Current treatments are sufficiently effective for only a minority of people with schizophrenia to lead an independent life, so the personal and societal costs of the disease are immense and terrible. The development of a broader theory of the illness and its possible genetic connections may thus lead to better diagnosis and treatment. It seems that genetic factors may lead to a predisposition to schizophrenia, but environmental factors probably nudge people into the illness or shield them from it.

See also Dementia, Dopamine, Frontal Lobes, Glutamate, Limbic System

Schwann Cells. *See* Glia

Second Messenger

Neurotransmitters are a first messenger. Second messengers are a class of molecules synthesized within a neuron that functionally link a message from a neurotransmitter with the internal cellular mechanisms that will subsequently initiate the message transmitted to other neurons in the sequence. Think of delivering a package to an office, where someone then relays it to the appropriate person or department.

See also Neuron, Neurotransmitter

Semantic Memory. *See* Memory

Semantics. *See* Language

Semipermeable Membrane. *See* Membrane

Sensitization. *See* Habituation

Sensory Lobes

Three paired lobes that comprise the posterior regions of the two cerebral hemispheres—the occipital (vision), temporal (sound), and parietal (touch) lobes. The lobes process the relevant incoming sensory information and integrate it into a unified perceptual map of the current situation. They also carry out many other functions associated with thought, memory, and language. See Figure 6.

See also Cerebral Cortex, Cerebral Hemispheres, Occipital Lobes, Parietal Lobes, Temporal Lobes

Sensory System

The body and brain systems that receive initially unconnected meaningless environmental information and begin the process of translating it into complex forms of integrated cognitive knowledge. We can also functionally consider the system as a communicative device that sends information about ourselves to others.

Gathering Sensory Information. We can sequence our sense organs by their reach for information, from those that gather information inside our body to those that reach out well beyond our body. The air and fluids coursing through our body's complex systems of tubes carry a wide variety of life-sustaining and life-threatening substances. Our body's immune system identifies and destroys bacterial and viral antigens, and our brain's hypothalamus maintains internal stability (homeostasis) by monitoring and regulating the concentrations of a variety of life-sustaining molecules in our body fluids.

Our tongue is appropriately located right below our nose and eyes. We can view it as a protective trapdoor that provides a final taste check on food before it enters our 30-foot-long digestive system. Its receptors monitor two chemical properties that are necessary to life (salt, sweet) and two that signal danger (sour, bitter). Other sensory receptors in our tongue, teeth, and mouth provide important information on the temperature, texture, and hardness of the food we plan to eat.

The large waterproof mantle of skin that covers our body looks inward to help keep our insides in place and to keep heat in and infection out. But it also looks outward to report on the weather and on the shape and size of the things we touch.

If our tongue and skin were our only sense organs, we would walk right past food we didn't touch or walk right into danger, so it's important to have other senses that let us know what's in the vicinity before we actually touch it.

Our sense of smell alerts us to nearby objects and organisms through molecules they release into the air that attach to receptors in our nose. Because odors travel through the air, we can tell that the source of the odor is in the vicinity, but we may have trouble locating it by smell alone, and smell provides no information on size and shape.

Vision and hearing solve such problems in that they permit our brain to locate objects at a distance—in the daylight and unobstructed and in the dark or obstructed. The doubling of eyes and ears adds sensory depth, enhancing our brain's ability to create an external impression of the object at its location, a significant sensory advantage. Vision and hearing are the only senses that allow our brain to psychologically leave its skull. We see and hear the object or event at the location, and not inside our brain where all cognition really takes place.

Sending Useful Information. Our sense organs bring important information into our brain, but they also communicate many things about ourselves and our values to other people. The typically visible parts of our skin, hair, nails, and teeth are all dead tissue, but we expend inordinate time and energy in trying to make them look alive. Perhaps it's the mortician in us. We support entire industries dedicated to this cosmetic compulsion to attract the attention of others. We rearrange skin and teeth, trim hair and nails, wash with special soaps and creams, dab on sweet-smelling perfumes and deodorants. To no avail. What others see of us is dead. Life is within.

Nevertheless, we often use our skin and other sense organs both to communicate and to hide what's happening within our brain and body. We add cosmetics to increase or decrease our apparent age or to compensate for perceived shortcomings in our appearance. We use such built-in *facial cosmetics* as frowns, grins, and yawns to display our inner emotions. Our eyes *sparkle, look tired,* and *spit fire* (even though we would be hard-pressed to describe what *sparkling eyes* look like). We shout in anger and laugh in joy. We gently communicate our love through caresses and kisses.

Others can infer much about our race, gender, state of health, approximate age, occupation, habits, and values concerning cleanliness by carefully observing our head and hands (the two parts of our body we tend to leave uncovered). They can infer even more from our clothing, the principal extension of our skin. Like skin, most clothing is made of dead material (cotton, wool, leather, and chemical synthetics). Because clothing, jewelry, and glasses provide a far more communicative (and easily altered) tool than skin, we can use this second layer of skin to communicate even more of the values and vitality hidden within our brain and body. For example, military people in full uniform symbolically drape their entire professional biographies on their body.

Social categorization can arise out of such surface communication—the hurt that comes from racism and sexism, the help that comes from recognizing a police officer when we need one. Adolescents soon learn that the best way to keep adults at a distance is to wear bizarre clothing and hairstyles and to bombard adults with loud atonal music. Mass media and mass culture thus combine to set surface styles for people who want to identify a group—or to identify with a group.

Think also of a third layer of skin: house and classroom walls. Like skin and clothing, such walls keep our possessions in place, help to maintain a comfortable temperature, and protect us from danger. But they also communicate much about our values and ourselves. The furnishings that gradually fill our homes are histories of our lives. Some classroom walls are filled with marvelous curricular windows that explore the world beyond the walls and with curricular mirrors that reflect values and activities back on the teachers and students. Some walls communicate excitement. Some invite touching. Some breathe life. Others just stand there, a stack of dead building materials.

See also Hearing, Sight, Smell, Taste, Touch

Septum

One of several systems (including the hypothalamus and nucleus accumbens) that process feelings of pleasure. The septum is located between the corpus callosum (that connects the two hemispheres) and the underlying fornix (that connects the hippocampus and hypothalamus). See Figure 7.

See also Corpus Callosum, Fornix, Hypothalamus, Nucleus Accumbens

Serotonin

A monoamine neurotransmitter associated with self-esteem levels that emerge out of one's ability to move smoothly and confidently. Serotonin inhibits quick impulsive movements, and so enhances smooth relaxed movements.

Serotonin (hydroxytryptamine, or 5-HT) is synthesized out of the amino acid tryptophan in the brainstem's raphe nuclei, from which it is widely distributed throughout the brain. The serotonin in our brain is only a small part of our body's total store of serotonin. Serotonin also regulates such body functions as intestinal contractions, cardiovascular functions, and endocrine secretions. Serotonin levels can be increased through exercise (which enhances movement control) and positive social feedback (which helps to elevate one's self-esteem). Many people suffering from plummeting self-esteem and serotonin levels have improved their lot with fluoxetine antidepressent drugs (such as Prozac, Zoloft, and Paxil).

When neurotransmitters leave an axon terminal, they attach to a receptor on the receiving neuron and pass on the sending neuron's chemical message. Most are then reabsorbed into the axon terminal and used again. Drugs such as Prozac block the reuptake channels on the terminal and thus slow the reabsorption process. This means that the serotonin neurotransmitters in the synapse may activate several times before being reabsorbed, and so fluoxetine drugs increase the effectiveness of a limited discharge of serotonin without actually increasing the amount in our brain.

Because movement is so central to our life, our ability to move confidently and smoothly (rather than fearfully and awkwardly) strongly affects our own level of self-esteem and also the way that others view us. High levels of serotonin are associated with high self-esteem and social status, and low levels with low self-esteem and social status. Behaviorally, high serotonin levels are associated with the calm assurance that leads to smoothly controlled movements, and low levels are associated with the irritability that leads to impulsive, uncontrolled, reckless, aggressive, and violent behaviors that are often directed to inappropriate targets and to suicidal tendencies.

See also Brainstem, Depression, Neuron, Neurotransmitter, Nucleus, Raphe Nuclei, Synapse

Sexuality. *See* Gender

Sight

The cognitive ability to create an internal, three-dimensional, color image of *what* is *where* in the continuously flowing external environment.

The site of 70% of our body's sensory receptors, our eyes begin the cognitive process of transforming reflected light into a mental

146 How to Explain a Brain

image of the objects that reflected the light. Light rays (photons) enter an eye through the system of cornea, iris, and lens, which focuses the image on the thin three-layer retinal sheet at the rear of the one-ounce eyeball. The retina is technically a part of the brain.

The rays are absorbed by the retina's 6 million cones and 120 million rods, with each cellular cone and rod focusing on a small, specific segment of the visual field. The centrally located cones (in the half-millimeter-wide fovea) process focused foreground information—the clearly lit, detailed, colored elements of an image (what something is). The peripherally located rods process the contextual or background information—the dimly lit, peripheral, black-gray-white, moving elements of the image (where something is located). The rich color spectrum we see results from the combined actions of only three kinds of cones that respond to red, blue, and green wavelengths.

The light waves absorbed by a rod or cone cause a chemical reaction that stimulates related retinal neurons to begin the process of combining the input of individual receptors into a complex image. In effect, the retina takes a rapid and continuous series of still pictures of the eye's visual field (much like a motion picture, which is made up of a rapidly projected sequence of still pictures that create the illusion of movement).

Our visual system is designed to focus our brain's attention principally on movement and contrast (lines, edges, contours, spots), and generally to monitor or ignore static solid areas. Thus, written languages are composed of meaningful combinations of vertical, horizontal, diagonal, and curved lines that move our focus along the line rather than rest it on one word.

The 1.2 million axon fibers in each eye's optic nerve use specialized parallel pathways to transmit a summary of the vast amount of visual data that the 126 million rods and cones receive. The rapid magnocellular pathway carries background, peripheral, movement, and depth information, and the slower parvocellular pathway carries foreground, focused, shape, and color information. Half of the optic fibers from each eye cross over to the opposite side of our brain, joining the remaining fibers from the other eye and continuing on to the lateral geniculate nucleus in the thalamus, our brain's initial sensory-processing area and relay center (located in the middle of our brain). Thus, each side of our brain received visual information from both eyes.

The information is next relayed to the amygdala for emotional analysis and to the visual cortex, two credit-card-sized areas in the occipital lobes at the back of our brain. The columns of neurons in the visual cortex are arranged to respond to specific patterns of lines, angles, and movements in the visual field. Further processing that occurs forward in the cerebral cortex combines line segments into shapes, colors them, combines them, locates them in space, names them, and contemplates their meanings. At this point, sensory processes are being transformed into perceptual and thought processes.

Think of your eyes as the projector lens and your visual cortex as the screen that registers the rapid sequence of sunlight-to-starlight still pictures it has received from your retina—still pictures that it translates into a continuous mental motion picture. Think of your frontal lobe neurons as the audience watching, interpreting, and responding to the film.

See also Cerebral Cortex, Retina, Sensory System, Thalamus

Sleep

An active but unconscious resting process. "Oh sleep! It is a gentle thing, beloved from pole to pole." Coleridge

We do happily sleep away one third of our life, and dreams dominate two of our eight sleeping hours—but why we do both continues to be something of a mystery. Rapid-eye-movement (REM) sleep and the structure of DNA were both discovered in 1953, but discoveries in genetics have since escalated while our understanding of sleeping and dreaming in humans and animals remains elusive (albeit with promise of important developments).

Current theories of the purpose of sleeping and dreaming generally incorporate the need to restore depleted molecules or damaged tissue, conserve energy, process information (such as memory), and avoid predators. It's important to detour the traffic off a road that's being repaired, and it's similarly important to shut down interference from our sensorimotor systems while our brain carries out necessary maintenance tasks. Several brain structures and melatonin fluctuations regulate our biological clock's approximately 24-hour circadian rhythm.

Our nightly sleeping-dreaming cycle incorporates four to six approximately 90-minute periods. Each period includes two sequential states. The states alternate between (1) a mid-to-deep sleep state characterized by slow synchronized delta wave activity, followed by (2) a more active brainstem-initiated REM sleep state in which much of our brain wave activity resembles an awake state. During this state, eyeballs move rapidly, body movement is inhibited, and male and female genitals are aroused. REM sleep is more prevalent in infant than in adult sleep, and so it may be developmentally important. Non-REM sleep is characterized by reduced activity in such regulatory functions as circulation and respiration, but increased activity in the production and release of hormones.

Glycogen, found in glial cells, is a molecule that especially interests sleep researchers. It's the stored form of glucose, the brain's energy source. Like gas in a car, glycogen stores are depleted by activity, and so must be replenished during nonactive periods (such as sleep or naps) during which sensorimotor activity is inhibited. The complex chemical replenishing process requires periods of brain activity but not wakefulness, and this may help to explain the nature of REM sleep.

Dreaming continues to be enigmatic, although earlier Freudian views of primal meanings are giving way to biological explanations. Most dreaming occurs during REM sleep, and scientists have noted increased activity in brain areas that process vision and emotion during dreaming and decreased activity in areas that process rational thought and attention. This tends to concur with the emotional, visual, irrational, distorted content of dreams. Dreaming may thus give our normally rational brain an opportunity to imagine and test solutions to life's problems without being inhibited by rational thought, and this unconscious exploration may enhance subsequent conscious creativity.

Sleeping and dreaming may also play an ill-understood role in the consolidation, editing, and erasing of memories (and especially procedural or skill memories). Memory formation and editing involve synaptic alterations in the neural networks involved in processing a memory, and such alterations are more easily effected during periods in which a brain isn't consciously active in thought and behavior.

Biological studies of sleeping and dreaming states have led to the development of medical interventions for various sleep disorders, and we can anticipate more success in this in the years ahead.

See also Brain Waves, Circadian Rhythm, Consciousness, Glucose, Melatonin, Memory, Suprachiasmatic Nuclei

Smell

The sensory system that recognizes various properties of airborne chemicals that enter our nose.

Our nose (situated right above the entrance to our digestive system) processes our sense of smell through two postage-stamp-sized mucus membranes at the top of the nasal air passages. The 400 types of receptors in the membranes encompass 40 million olfactory receptor cells that send hairlike projections into the mucus. These receptors interact with odor-bearing molecules that have entered our nose and are trapped and dissolved within the mucus. Smell receptors are bare neural endings, so when we smell something, our brain is in direct chemical contact with the outside environment. The neurons projecting into the mucus membrane regenerate themselves every few weeks. Furthermore, each person has a unique combination of receptors, so we each take in a different bouquet of smells from the environment.

Only a small amount of the air we breathe passes over these receptors, but our sense of smell is powerful enough to respond to very light concentrations of odor-bearing molecules. Most animals have a much more powerful and directional sense of smell than we have.

Perhaps 30 molecules are involved in the 10,000 or so different odors we can recognize. Most odors are combinations of molecules that enter our nose in the air we breathe and then attach to receptors. It's difficult to classify smells, but seven primary odors have been identified: minty (peppermint), floral (roses), ethereal (unscented nail polish), musky (musk), resinous (camphor), acrid (vinegar), and putrid (rotten eggs).

Smell is the only sense that doesn't pass through the thalamus. The olfactory bulbs, the initial odor-processing center, have major connections to the amygdala and temporal lobes. Smell plays an important role in the formation and recall of emotion-laden memories, but we can't recall the odor of an absent object (such as the odor of an orange or a rose) in the same way that we can recall their shape and color. Smell is more important than taste in our recognition and selection of many foods.

See also Pheromone, Sensory System

Somatosensory Cortex

A narrow band in the anterior part of the sensory lobes (just behind the motor cortex) devoted to touch sensations received from various body parts.

Think of a two-inch-wide band stretching across the top of our brain from ear to ear—the left side receiving touch sensations from the right side of our body, and the right side receiving touch sensations from the left side of our body—and we're represented upside down. The areas at the top of our brain receive sensations from our feet and the areas by our ears from our face. The amount of somatosensory cortex space devoted to a part of the body is related to the level of sensitivity to touch that's needed and not to the size of the body part. The face and hands thus receive the most space because both are very sensitive to touch.

Check it out with the two points of a compass (or two pins) that are perhaps a quarter of an inch apart. Touch your lips and fingertips with the points, and you'll feel both of them, but touch your leg or back with the two points, and you'll probably feel only one point, because fewer receptors are in those areas. See Figure 10.

See also Homunculus, Motor Cortex

Somatostatin

A peptide that regulates the release of insulin and inhibits intestinal secretions and growth hormone.

See also Neurotransmitter

Sound. *See* Hearing

Spindle Neuron

A large, cigar-shaped type of neuron usually found in the fifth layer of the frontal lobes and only in humans and higher primates.

Our 100,000 spindle neurons (or spindle cells) are massively interconnected with other brain regions and seem to play a key role in rapidly processing information and behavior related to complex social emotions. We thus instantly know how to respond to close friends, and we typically have a well-developed sense of morality and ethics that we activate when suddenly confronted with moral and ethical challenges. See Figure 3.

See also Cerebral Cortex, Neuron

Spine. *See* Neuron

Stellate Cell. *See* Cerebellum, Cerebral Cortex

Stem Cells

Immature cells that initially can reproduce and develop into any type of body or brain cell—typically, the kind of cells prevalent in the area where the stem cell is located.

The discovery of stem cells is an important recent scientific development. Stem cells can serve both as a research tool and as a potential implant treatment for people who have maladies such as leukemia, Parkinson's disease, and Huntington's disease. The implanted stem cells divide and assume the tasks of the damaged or lost cells, thus hastening recovery. Stem cells have become a controversial issue, however, because aborted embryos are currently perhaps the best source for viable stem cells.

See also Cell, Cognitive and Motor Degeneration

Steroid Hormones. *See* Hormones

Stimulus

Anything that can activate sensory receptors and thought processes or influence the direction of a behavioral response.

See also Conditioning, Habituation

Stress

A condition in which a looming real or imagined challenge physically or psychologically overwhelms a person. A stress response is the sequence of biological events that are triggered by the stressor.

Our brain is on constant alert for potential dangers and opportunities, and it can, under most conditions, successfully respond—from successfully crossing a street to skiing down a mountain, from growing a garden to cooking a meal. Prior related successful experience and general problem-solving skills often provide a necessary useful edge.

The response dynamics often change when we confront novel or serious emotionally charged challenges that require an immediate response—a rapidly approaching car, a fleeting opportunity for a lot of free strawberries on a hot busy day. The challenge, then, is to respond quickly and decisively on the basis of the limited available facts, because when survival or the prompt processing of food is at stake, a rapid (even if it's not the best possible) response is preferable to informed death or spoilage from delay.

So if our brain assesses the challenge as nonimminent, something that can be solved through reflective processes and established strategies, we will follow that rational route—and do so in most of the challenges we face daily. Conversely, if our brain needs but doesn't have an immediate solution, it typically activates its reflexive stress response. The amygdala and related systems signal the hypothalamus, which signals the pituitary gland, which signals the adrenal glands (above the kidneys), which release cortisol and other hormones into the bloodstream. It's an automatic response pattern that will principally use innate fight/flight response programs.

The reflexive stress response increases the blood rate to move needed nutrients and hormones rapidly throughout our body and brain, increases the activity of the large fight/flight muscle groups by diverting energy away from currently low-priority muscle groups (such as in the stomach—why process food when we might die?), and reduces energy normally allocated to the immune system (again, not a current high priority when a car is rapidly approaching). Furthermore, hormones such as cortisol inhibit currently low-priority reflective activity—something we've all experienced when we made a stupid mistake while we were stressed.

Rapid reflexive responses may thus save our life, but they can also unfortunately lead to the stereotyping (such as in racism, sexism, elitism), regrets, and apologies that are unfortunately so common when we make fearful, impulsive, and inappropriate stress-driven responses on the basis of limited superficial information. Worse, the neurotransmitter and hormonal discharges associated with fear can strengthen the emotional and weaken the factual memories of an event if the stressful situation is serious or chronic. We thus become fearful of something, but we're often not sure why, so we've learned little from the experience that's consciously useful (because a reflexive stress response occurs unconsciously, and so reduces our ability to create factual memories).

Furthermore, the oversecretion of powerful stress hormones (such as cortisol) that accompanies the chronic activation of our reflexive stress pathways can physically deteriorate key areas of our factual memory and reflective systems. As suggested earlier, because the point of a stress response is to respond quickly, it's important for our emotion and attention system to turn up the reflexive pathways and to turn down the reflective pathways that would delay the response. The stress hormones enhance the functioning of reflexive pathways, but they can negatively affect the robustness of chronically turned-down reflective pathways.

So what we have is a powerful and useful stress-driven reflexive response system that should be activated in situations that require an immediate forceful response, such as the sudden accelerations and rapid braking often necessary in adverse traffic conditions. The reflexive system evolved, however, to be used as a temporary rather than continuous response system (continuous acceleration and braking when driving is not advisable). So it's like salt: A little bit of it is biologically useful; a whole lot is generally harmful.

The stress response evolved to deal with physical dangers and opportunities, but much contemporary stress emerges out of perceived social challenges that don't require such an immediate high-voltage response. Stress-related illnesses have thus become a serious contemporary health threat. Schools enhance our society's quality of life when they teach students how to analyze the challenges they face and to reflectively solve those that should be reflectively solved.

A rich literature on stress-reduction strategies has emerged over the years. In effect, it suggests the need to develop the following three general categories of beliefs and skills. It's good, simple advice, but not necessarily easy to implement:

1. *You*. View change and challenge as a constant in life and welcome them as a chance to grow. Approach potentially stressful challenges with a clear sense of the importance of your own personal goals, values, and abilities. Realize that you can't do everything, and so focus on what you must do and ignore or seek help for the things you can't or shouldn't do.

2. *Others*. We're a social species, and so we appropriately seek help from others, and help those who need our help. It's thus important to commit strongly to the significant relationships in your life. Identify the relationship between major potentially stressful challenges and your own clearly defined personal, family, friendship, and career priorities. Separate the foreground/background and subjective/objective elements of a challenge. Don't take things personally that weren't meant to be personal slights, and don't take work problems home or bring personal problems to work.

3. *Responsibility*. Develop an internal rather than external locus of control, which means that although others may have caused your problem, it's now your problem, so assume the responsibility for solving it as best you can. Don't consider yourself to be a victim of circumstances, but seek to take personal control of your life, with all its attendant successes and failures.

See also Amygdala, Anxiety, Cortisol, Hormones, Hypothalamus, Locus of Control

Reference

Sapolsky, R. (1998). *Why zebras don't get ulcers: An updated guide to stress, stress-related diseases, and coping.* New York: Freeman.

Striatum. *See* Basal Ganglia

Subcortical

The part of the brain that lies below the large, deeply folded cerebral cortex. This region includes the hindbrain, midbrain, thalamus, and cerebellum. See Figures 5, 7, 8, and 11.

See also Brain, Cerebral Cortex, Cerebrum

Substance P

An 11-amino-acid peptide distributed widely in the central and peripheral nervous systems. It transmits pain messages to the brain and so helps to initiate and regulate emotions.

See also Central Nervous System, Neuron, Peripheral Nervous System

Substantia Nigra

Paired nuclei in the finger-sized brainstem's midbrain section (the top one inch). These nuclei produce and then project dopamine into basal ganglia and frontal lobe areas. Dopamine networks are involved in planning and regulating movement.

The substantia nigra is functionally a part of the basal ganglia, which is composed of five subcortical structures that play key relay roles in regulating the smooth progression of movements and in processing emotion. Substantia nigra means *black substance* in Latin, and a pigment in the substantia nigra neurons give them their dark color.

Extensive cell death in the substantia nigra results in Parkinson's disease, the gradual loss of conscious movement regulation and other frontal lobe functions. See Figures 5 and 7.

See also Basal Ganglia, Dopamine, Midbrain

Sulcus (SUL-kus)

Any of the many fissures or furrows in the deeply folded cerebral cortex.

Think of a sulcus as a narrow valley between two close hills. Crumble a sheet of paper to demonstrate how a large surface area can be compressed into a small space through such convolutions. Perhaps the best-known brain sulci are the central sulcus (between the sensory and frontal lobes) and the longitudinal fissure (between the two hemispheres). See Figure 9.

See also Cerebral Cortex, Gyrus

Suprachiasmatic Nuclei (supra-KIE-as-matic)

A pair of small pacemaker nuclei in the hypothalamus that receive information from the retina on the intensity of external light. This information helps regulate various circadian rhythms (such as to synchronize sleep with darkness). Suprachiasmatic means that it's located just above (supra) the optic chiasm (chiasmatic) where axons from our two eyes cross on their way to the occipital lobe. See Figures 7 and 8.

See also Circadian Rhythm, Hypothalamus, Occipital Lobes, Sleep

Synapse (SIN-apse)

The narrow gap (or cleft) between the axon terminal (or bouton) of a presynaptic neuron and the dendritic or cellular receptors on the postsynaptic neuron. Neurotransmitters released from the presynaptic neuron's terminal diffuse across the synaptic gap and attach to receptors on the postsynaptic neuron, thus carrying molecular information from one neuron to another. One cubic millimeter of cortical tissue will contain more than 200 million synapses. See Figures 1 and 2.

See also Neuron, Neurotransmitter, Postsynaptic Neuron, Presynaptic Neuron

Synesthesia (sin-es-THEE-zhuh)

A condition in which (about 1 in 200) people combine or confuse certain sensory modalities rather than keep them separate—probably because of neuronal misconnection or the cross-activation of the relevant sensory system networks.

A person with synesthesia thus might associate specific colors with specific musical tones or specific taste sensations with specific tactile experiences. But even people without synesthesia speak of singing the blues and noting the sharp taste of certain cheeses, so combining and confusing sensory modalities is perhaps something we all do at some level. The angular gyrus is a region in the cerebral cortex where various discrete sensory concepts are combined into more complex concepts, and so it's perhaps a viable candidate for the site of synesthesic sensations.

The ability to combine seemingly unrelated concepts is central to metaphor and creativity, and so synesthesia may be positively related to creativity.

See also Angular Gyrus, Sensory System

Syntax. *See* Language

T

Taste

Our final sensory check on the palatability of food before it enters our digestive system, integrally associated with the adjoining sense of smell.

Our tongue is a four-inch-long slab of muscle with 9,000 taste buds arranged in groups of about 100 on raised projections (papillae) located mostly on the perimeter of its upper surface. There are also 10,000 taste buds located on our palate, inner cheeks, throat, and tonsils. Because taste receptors (like smell receptors) are in direct, unprotected contact with the environment, they function for only about 10 days before being replaced. Taste sensations are sent (via the medulla and thalamus) to the insula in the cerebral cortex for analysis.

Taste buds report only on food that is soluble in water, so saliva is necessary for our sense of taste. The front of our tongue is the principal processor of the sweet and salty tastes of foods that help our body maintain proper levels of glucose and sodium, which are important to our brain's metabolic and information-processing functions. The back part of our tongue processes sour and bitter tastes (a final check on toxins and spoiled food). Our tongue and mouth also register temperature, touch, and pain, and our teeth register hardness. Although our brain receives these messages separately from taste, it combines the total sensory message of taste and smell into a complex integrated flavor sensation—smooth hot chocolate or crunchy peanut brittle. The early maturation of this important sensory integration is evident in the behavior of infants who examine almost everything they pick up by putting it into their mouth. Fetal taste buds respond to amniotic fluid chemicals by the third trimester.

Our sense of taste is as social as it is biological in that we generally prefer to eat and drink with others. Eating and drinking are major elements in many celebratory and romantic events, even though the basic biological process involves little more than pouring a daily ration of about two gallons of food and water into our 30-foot digestive tube. Eating is generally much more than taste. It's a rich mix of all the senses and sociability—the cooking aromas, the tactile crunch of celery and apples, the attractiveness of the food on the table, the sounds of popcorn popping, and the flow of conversation.

Most people eagerly select from a wide range of tastes and textures, even though a cynic may suggest that it all comes down to little more than variations on pizza—some variation of bread with a topping—whether it's called a sandwich, pancake, crepe, pie, layer cake, or lasagna; or whether it's sliced and shaped into Chinese noodles or Italian pasta. We thus celebrate similarity and diversity when we eat—with each other, with all our senses.

It's probably also important to realize that although the taking in of food and drink to initiate the digestive process tends to be social, celebratory, and often romantic, the inevitable conclusion of the process tends to be solitary and neither celebratory nor romantic. Our language is rich with terms that describe and laud eating and drinking, but the terms for defecation and urination are often euphemistic or considered vulgar—and the processes themselves often seem part of our shame culture. Furthermore, males and females easily eat together in a restaurant, but they use separate restrooms.

It's interesting to muse beyond food and drink input and output to the social, celebratory, and romantic taking in of culture and information (such as in concerts, theaters, and schools) and to the shame that we associate with the things we discard because the system couldn't assimilate them—the compositions and plays that aren't performed, the students who failed, the sports teams that lost.

See also Brainstem, Insula, Sensory System, Smell, Thalamus

Telencephalon. *See* Forebrain

Temperament

An innate lifelong initial emotional response bias to environmental challenges.

A person's temperament emerges early in life and typically centers somewhere along a continuum between bold/uninhibited and anxious/inhibited, with boldness processed principally in the left hemisphere and anxiousness in the right hemisphere.

Temperament is a useful human trait that allows us to initiate a response quickly and confidently. The bold tend to go forward in curiosity (sensing an opportunity); the anxious tend to go backward in hesitant concern (sensing danger). Because we frequently follow our developing temperamental bias, we tend to become quite competent with it over time. For example, bold people tend to become skilled at responding boldly (similar to handedness, which develops exceptional competence with the favored hand).

Temperament variations don't imply that one type of temperament is superior. Our society profits from the strengths of those who are typically either cautious or bold (such as investors who specialize in either conservative or risky investments). Indeed, opposite temperaments often marry each other, and the relationship generally profits from the strengths of each (if they both respect their partner's temperament) because life confronts us with both dangers and opportunities. School groups often exhibit a similar temperament range—from staff and students who are stimulated by any novel idea to those who feel threatened by any change.

See also Emotion and Feelings

Temporal Lobes

Paired sensory lobes in the upper back section of the cerebral cortex that participate in the recognition of dangers and opportunities—focusing especially on hearing, smell, taste, language and music perception and comprehension, higher visual processing (such as face and object recognition), and memory.

Imagine an ear-to-ear line across your skull. The occipital, temporal, and parietal sensory lobes of the cerebral cortex are principally located in the back (above the thalamus), and the frontal lobes are in the front (above the basal ganglia). The temporal lobes are located between the occipital and frontal lobes and below the parietal lobes, and encompass 22% of the cerebral cortex.

The back-to-front organizing principle of both the cortical and subcortical areas is that the brain's back section recognizes and creates mental models of dangers and opportunities, and the front section manipulates and transforms these models into a response that it then initiates. See Figures 6 and 8.

See also Basal Ganglia, Cerebral Cortex, Cerebral Hemispheres, Cerebrum, Frontal Lobes, Hearing, Occipital Lobes, Parietal Lobes, Thalamus

Thalamus

A key relay station in processing all the senses, except the sense of smell.

The thalamus is composed of two golf-ball-sized structures located deep within the cerebral hemispheres. It's divided into many specialized nuclei that initially analyze the sensory information that passes through the thalamus. For example, the lateral geniculate nucleus processes visual information from the retina, and the medial geniculate nucleus processes auditory information from the inner ear. The pulvinar located at the back of the thalamus plays an important role in regulating visual attention.

The thalamus also receives projections from the basal ganglia, cerebellum, and cerebral cortex, so it's involved in many cognitive functions. The cherry-sized hypothalamus located below the thalamus is directly or indirectly involved in just about every body regulatory activity, so the two structures are central to the brain in both their location and function. See Figures 7 and 8.

See also Basal Ganglia, Cerebellum, Cerebral Cortex, Hypothalamus, Sensory System

Theta Waves. *See* Brain Waves

Threshold

The level of intensity necessary for a stimulus to elicit sensory awareness or to cross an acceptable–unacceptable line.

We must continually determine the point at which one quality becomes another as we confront life's challenges. To determine whether something is true or false is an absolute (veridical) decision—something like an off/on switch, such as that 6×5 is always 30. To determine whether something is right or wrong, fair or unfair, appropriate or inappropriate, pleasant or unpleasant, beautiful or ugly, and so on, is more a matter of opinion or preference (an adaptive decision)—and it's more like a dimmer switch.

Although we constantly make both veridical and adaptive decisions, the acceptable threshold setting of most adaptive decisions can vary from day to day, from situation to situation. For example, we might happily do something on Tuesday that we would have avoided on Monday. Our frontal lobes play a key role in making these constantly shifting and intellectually stimulating decisions.

At the neuronal level, the *threshold* is the level at which the incoming molecular messages are sufficiently strong to trigger an outgoing message (an action potential).

See also Frontal Lobes

Touch

Our sensory awareness of the external environment through its direct physical contact with the mantle of skin that covers our body.

Our skin has more than a half million nerve endings that provide our brain with immediate information on just about anything that touches our body, even a mosquito landing. Our hand has 1,300 nerve endings per square inch. Across our body, a patch of skin the size of a quarter averages more than 3 million cells, 250 sensory receptors, 100 sweat glands, 50 nerve endings, and three feet of blood vessels. Our body's six-pound, 20-square-foot, two-layer mantle of skin is the largest and least compact of our sense organs. Although the other sense organs are only inches away from our brain, information from the skin on our feet travels several feet to reach our brain.

Note time and distance differences in the movement of touch information by tapping your nose with your index finger and note whether you felt the tap principally in your nose or your finger. Then use the same finger to tap your ankle, and again note whether you principally felt the tap in your finger or ankle. The chances are good that you felt the tap on your nose rather than on your finger, and on your finger rather than on your ankle because your nose is closer to your brain than to your finger, but your finger is closer to your brain than to your ankle.

The epidermis is the constantly renewing outside layer of our skin. It replaces itself about once a month, as living cells gradually move to the surface, where they form a hard waterproof cover about 15 cells thick. Protective oils keep the cells pliable, but the top layers constantly flake off.

The dermis is our skin's thicker inside layer. It contains nerve endings, hair roots, sweat and oil glands, and blood vessels. Fibroelastic tissue allows our skin to maintain its tight, smooth cover, and a layer of fatty tissue beneath the dermis attaches the skin to our body. This layer of fat also provides an emergency food supply, acts as insulation to conserve body heat, and cushions our body from bumps and blows.

Various specialized receptors register variations in skin temperature and pressure. Our skin has about 10 times more cold receptors than hot receptors. Some receptors respond to intense pressure and others to gentle stroking. Receptors located adjacent to hair roots monitor hair movements.

Pain is initially useful because it alerts us to a threat, which can result from intense changes in temperature and pressure from skin cuts. We subjectively perceive pain as sharp, dull, throbbing, or shooting and do what we can to turn it off, once we've responded to the problem. Our brain produces endorphin peptides to reduce intense pain, and we've developed many drugs to reduce or eliminate it.

Touch information and motor output are initially processed in the somatosensory and motor cortexes, two narrow bands of neural tissue that spread from ear to ear across the cerebral cortex, but many other brain areas also participate in these important tasks.

The lengthy human birth process that squeezes the body through a relatively narrow birth canal helps to activate our skin as a functioning organ. The postbirth licking that many animal mothers give to their more easily delivered young serves the same function. Our sense of touch develops early and is stimulated by a child's gentle and positive contact with the surrounding environment—by cuddling and hugging, modeling clay, running in the breeze, playing catch, finger painting, taking things apart, and putting them together. Children must physically interact with objects in their environment to understand them, and the school can make a major contribution to this development through hands-on activities. Tactile stimulation is like rubbing the world on the outside layer of our brain.

See also Endorphin, Motor Cortex, Sensory System, Somatosensory Cortex

Tourette's Syndrome

A disorder related to obsessive-compulsive disorder that affects about 1 in 1,000 people, typically males. It's characterized by chronic motor tics and sometimes by involuntary speech tics that involve vulgar language. The disease seems to be genetically based, and its onset occurs before adulthood.

See also Obsessive-Compulsive Disorder

Transduction

The conversion of energy from one form into another (such as producing electrical power out of mechanical power).

Our retina transduces reflected light waves into neural impulses, and our auditory system transduces rhythmic sound patterns into speech and music. One could also metaphorically think of our brain as *transducing* motor neuron impulses into paintings and violin music. Our brain's cognitive representations of an external environment can thus be thought of as a metaphorical form of energy transduction.

V

Vagus Nerve

The longest cranial nerve—connecting our brainstem's medulla and our body's abdomen. It projects to all body organs involved in the regulation of parasympathetic nervous system survival functions (circulation, respiration, digestion). See Figure 5.

See also Neuron, Peripheral Nervous System

Vasopressin (vay-zo-PRESS-in)

A pituitary peptide that helps to regulate water retention and blood pressure. It also seems to enhance memory formation. Vasopressin and another pituitary peptide called oxytocin play key roles in enhancing social and bonding behaviors, especially between sexual mates and between parents and children. Oxytocin levels tend to be higher in females, and vasopressin levels tend to be higher in males.

See also Neuron, Neurotransmitter, Oxytocin, Pituitary Gland

Ventricle

A cavity within our body or brain. Our brain has four major cavities or ventricles that are filled with cerebrospinal fluid, which absorbs head movements to buffer our brain, and allows our gelatinous brain to float. One ventricle is located between the brainstem and the cerebellum, one is in the center of the brain, and two are located within the hemispheres. See Figures 5 and 7.

See also Vesicle

Vesicle

A small cavity or packet within a biological structure, such as the brain ventricles. The term *vesicle* is principally used in our brain to identify the packet of neurotransmitters in an axon terminal awaiting release into the synapse.

See also Neuron, Ventricle

Vision. *See* Sight

Vomeronasal Organ. *See* Pheromone

W

Wernicke's Area (VERN-ik-eez)

A language comprehension region located in the upper posterior (typically) left temporal lobe.

The German neurologist Carl Wernicke reported its discovery in the late 19th century following studies of specific speech comprehension problems of people who had lesions in this region. Wernicke's area is composed of a number of subsystems that process specific elements of language. See Figure 6.

See also Aphasia, Arcuate Fasciculus, Broca's Area, Planum Temporale

White Matter. *See* Cerebral Cortex

Working Memory. *See* Memory

Bibliography
and Resources

REFERENCES

Aunger, R. (2002). *The electric meme: A new theory of how we think.* New York: Free Press.

Black, I. (2001). *The dying of Enoch Wallace: Life, death, and the changing brain.* New York: McGraw-Hill.

Blackmore, S. (1999). *The meme machine.* New York: Oxford University Press.

Damasio, A. (1999). *The feeling of what happens: Body and emotion in the making of consciousness.* New York: Harcourt Brace.

Damasio, A. (2003). *Looking for Spinoza: Joy, sorrow and the feeling brain.* New York: Harcourt Brace.

Deasy, R. (Ed.). (2002). *Critical links: Learning in the arts and student academic and social development.* Wasington, DC: Council of Chief State School Officers (One Massachusetts Ave., NW, Suite 700, Washington, DC 20001-1431; www.aep-arts.org).

Gardner, H. (1983). *Frames of mind: The theory of multiple intelligences.* New York: Basic Books.

Marcus, G. (2004). *The birth of the mind: How a tiny number of genes creates the complexities of human thought.* New York: Basic Books.

Meltzoff, A., & Prinz, W. (2002). *The imitative mind: Development, evolution, and brain bases.* Cambridge, England: Cambridge University Press. (Note especially chapter 14 by the principal discoverers of mirror neurons, Giacomo Rizzolatti and Vittorio Gallese, "From Mirror Neurons to Imitation: Facts and Speculations," p. 247–266.)

Perkins, D. (1995). *Outsmarting I.Q.: The emerging theory of learnable intelligence.* New York: Free Press.

Ridley, M. (2000). *Genome: The autobiography of a species in 23 chapters.* New York: Perennial.

Rymer, R. (1993). *Genie: An abused child's flight from silence.* New York: HarperCollins.

Sapolsky, R. (1998). *Why zebras don't get ulcers: An updated guide to stress, stress-related diseases, and coping.* New York: Freeman.

Sternberg, R. (1996). *Successful intelligence: How practical and creative intelligence determine success in life.* New York: Simon & Schuster.

Strauch, B. (2003). *The primal teen: What the new discoveries about the teenage brain tell us about our kids.* New York: Doubleday.

BOOKS FOR GENERAL READERS

Ackerman, D. (2004). *An alchemy of mind: The marvel and mystery of the brain.* New York: Scribner.

Andreasen, N. (2001). *Brave new brain: Conquering mental illness in the era of the genome.* New York: Oxford.

Baron-Cohen, S. (2003). *The essential difference: The truth about the male and female brain.* New York: Basic Books.

Berninger, V., & Richards, T. (2002). *Brain literacy for educators and psychologists.* San Diego, CA: Academic Press.

Blackmore, S. (2004). *Consciousness: An introduction.* New York: Oxford.

Calvin, W. (2004). *A brief history of the mind: From apes to intellect and beyond.* New York: Oxford University Press.

Changeux, J.-P. (2004). *The physiology of truth: Neuroscience and human knowledge.* Cambridge, MA: Harvard University Press.

Corballis, M. (2002). *From hand to mouth: The origins of language.* Princeton, NJ: Princeton University Press.

Drumbach, D. (2000). *The brain explained.* Upper Saddle River, NJ: Prentice Hall.

Dubin, M. (2002). *How the brain works.* Malden, MA: Blackwell Science.

Edelman, G. (2004). *Wider than the sky: The phenomenal gift of consciousness.* New Haven, CT: Yale University Press.

Goldberg, E. (2001). *The executive brain: Frontal lobes and the civilized mind.* New York: Oxford.

Greenfield, S. (2000). *The private life of the brain.* New York: Wiley.

Jensen., E. (2004). *Teaching with the brain in mind.* Alexandria, VA: Association for Supervision and Curriculum Development.

Koch, C. (2004). *The quest for consciousness: A neurobiological approach.* Engelewood, CO: Roberts and Company.

Marcus, G. (2004). *The birth of the mind: How a tiny number of genes creates the complexities of human thought.* New York: Basic Books.

McGaugh, J. (2003). *Memory and emotion: The making of lasting memories.* New York: Columbia University Press.

Newberg, A., & D'Aquili, E. (2001). *Why God won't go away: Brain science and religious belief.* New York: Ballentine.

Pinker, S. (2002). *The blank slate: The modern denial of human nature.* New York: Viking.

Premack, D., & Premack, A. (2003). *Original intelligence: Unlocking the mystery of who we are.* New York: McGraw-Hill.

Provine, R. (2001). *Laughter: A scientific investigation.* New York: Viking.

Quartz, S., & Sejnowski, T. (2002). *Liars, lovers, and heroes: What the new brain science reveals about how we become who we are.* New York: Morrow.

Ratey, J. (2001). *A user's guide to the brain.* New York: Pantheon Books.

Restak, R. (2002). *The secret life of the brain.* Washington, DC: Joseph Henry Press.

Restak, R. (2003). *The new brain: How the modern age is rewiring your mind.* New York: Rodale.

Schacter, D. (2001). *The seven sins of memory: How the mind forgets and remembers.* New York: Houghton Mifflin.

Schwartz, J., & Begley, S. (2002). *The mind and the brain: Neuroplasticity and the power of mental force.* New York: HarperCollins.

Shaywitz, S. (2003). *Overcoming dyslexia: A new and complete science-based program for reading problems at any level.* New York: Knopf.

Solms, M., & Turnbull, O. (2002). *The brain and the inner world: An introduction to the neuroscience of subjective experience.* New York: Other Press.

Sousa, D. (2001). *How the brain learns.* Thousand Oaks, CA: Corwin Press.

Sylwester, R. (2003). *A biological brain in a cultural classroom: Enhancing cognitive and social development through collaborative classroom management.* Thousand Oaks, CA: Corwin Press.

Taylor, S. (2002). *The tending instinct: How nurturing is essential to who we are and how we live.* New York: Henry Holt.

Wolfe, P. (2001). *Brain matters: Translating research into classroom practice.* Alexandria, VA: Association for Supervision and Curriculum Development.

Zeman, A. (2002). *Consciousness: A user's guide.* New Haven, CT: Yale University Press.

MASS CIRCULATION MAGAZINES THAT OFTEN CONTAIN ARTICLES ON COGNITIVE NEUROSCIENCE DEVELOPMENTS

Discover Magazine
New Scientist
Newsweek
New Yorker
Psychology Today
Science News
Scientific American
Time Magazine
U.S. News & World Report

USEFUL WEB SITES THAT FOCUS ON COGNITIVE NEUROSCIENCE INFORMATION AND ISSUES

Brain Connection. *www.brainconnection.com*

Useful, nontechnical information on cognitive neuroscience issues for parents and educators. *Brain Connection* (click on "Web sites") contains extensive descriptive and analytical reviews of most of the following recommended Web sites.

BrainInfo Database. *braininfo.rprc.washington.edu/mainmenu.html*

A comprehensive resource on brain regions, terms, and processes.

Brainland: The Neuroscience Information Center. *www.brainland.com*

Professional information for the neuroscience community, but also quite a bit that's useful for educators interested in the neurosciences.

Brain and Mind: Electronic Magazine on Neuroscience. *www.epub. org/cm/home_i.htm*

Focused on neuroscience education issues but also useful for educators interested in the neurosciences.

The Child Development Institute. *www.cdipage.com*

Useful information for parents on problems children and adolescents confront.

Eric Chudler's Neuroscience Resource Site.
http://faculty.washington.edu/chudler/ehceduc.html

An informative Web site with links to many others. See also the listing that follows for Chudler's other Web site, *Neuroscience for Kids*.

CogNet: MIT Cognitive and Brain Science Community Online.
http://cognet.mit.edu

A wide range of useful information in an interactive format, sponsored by the Massachusetts Institute of Technology.

Cold Spring Harbor's DNA Learning Center.
http://vector.chsl.dnaftb

A fine multimedia introductory resource on genetics.

The Charles A. Dana Foundation. *www.dana.org*

A broad informative Web site suitable for both scientists and the general public. *Brainy Kids Online* is an especially useful section for educators.

Howard Hughes Medical Institute—Seeing, Hearing, and Smelling the World. *www.hhmi.org.senses*

A fine, nontechnical introduction to the sensory system.

Neuroguide.com. *www.neuroguide.com*

A comprehensive access to Internet Web sites on brain issues. See especially *Best Bets*.

NeurOn–Neurolab Online. *http://quest.arc.nasa.gov/nuron*

A report on NASA neurological research, with a focus on school use of the information.

Neuroscience for Kids. *http://faculty.washington.edu/chudler/neurok.html*

A marvelous resource of information and exploratory projects for young people. See also *Eric Chudler's Neuroscience Resource Site.*

New Horizons for Learning. *www.newhorizons.org*

A useful Web site intended for educators who are interested in the cognitive neurosciences and related educational issues.

Public Broadcasting Service Teacher Source. *www.pbs.org/teachersource*

Excellent resource for educators on many topics, including the cognitive neurosciences.

San Francisco's Exploratorium Online. *www.exploratorium.com*

An excellent Internet expansion of an excellent interactive museum.

The Society for Neuroscience. *www.sfn.org*

The Web site of the professional society, but *Brain Backgrounders* and *Brain Briefings* are especially useful resources for educators.

The Washington University School of Medicine Neuroscience Tutorial. *http://thalamus.wustl.edu/course*

An excellent Internet tutorial on the brain and brain anatomy.

Whole Brain Atlas. *www.med.harvard.edu/AANLIB/home.html*

It's just what the title says—anything you could possibly want to know.

The World Wide Web Virtual Library: Neuroscience (Biosciences). *http://neuro.med.cornell.edu/VL*

Links to just about any Web site one could imagine.

Index

Broca's aphasia, 20
Broca's area, 9, 36–37
Brodmann areas, 37

Catecholamine, 38
Caudate nucleus, 11, 29.
     See also Basal ganglia
Cell
   description of, 38–39
   nucleus of, 122
Central nervous system,
     39–40, 114–115
Cerebellum, 9–10, 40
Cerebral cortex
   composition of, 41
   description of, 41
   layers of, 41
   metaphors for, 42–43
   regions of, 9
Cerebral hemispheres, 7, 14, 43–45
Cerebrospinal fluid, 164–165
Cerebrum, 45
Children
   cognitive development of, 78
   growth and development
        of, 76–79
   hearing by, 80–81
   with language learning delay, 81
   love by, 95
Cholecystokinin, 45
Cholinergic, 46
Cingulate gyrus, 10–11, 46
Circadian rhythm, 46–47
Circulatory system, 47–48
Classical conditioning, 51
Cochlea, 48, 80
Codons, 56
Cognition, 48
Cognitive degeneration, 49–50
Cognitive development, 78
Cognitive neuroscience, 35
Commissure
   anterior, 10, 19
   definition of, 19
Computerized imaging technology,
     33–34
Conditioning, 51

Consciousness
   core, 52–53
   description of, 51–52
   extended, 53
   protoself and, 52
Coronal plane, 7, 12
Corpus callosum, 10, 54
Cortisol, 54
Creative intelligence, 88
*Critical Links: Learning in the
     Arts and Student Academic
     and Social Development,* 23–24

Declarative memory, 100
Delta waves, 36
Dendrite, 4, 116
Deoxyribonucleic acid, 55–56
Depolarization, 116
Depression, 57
Dermis, 162
Diencephalon, 68, 86
DNA. *See* Deoxyribonucleic acid
Dopamine, 31, 57–58, 140
Dreaming, 147–148
Drugs, 58–60
Dura mater, 103
Dyslexia, 20

Ear, 48, 80
Electroencephalogram
   brain waves identified on, 36
   description of, 33–34
   evoked potential, 66
Emotion
   definition of, 61
   feelings vs., 61–62
   types of, 62–63, 132
Emotional arousal, 19, 25,
     61–62, 100
Empathy, 64
Endocrine glands, 65
Endorphin, 65, 120–121,
     162–163
Engram, 65
Enzyme, 65
Epidermis, 162
Epinephrine, 15, 66, 122

Lesion, 93
Limbic system, 61, 93–94
Lobes, of hemispheres, 45
Locus ceruleus, 94, 122
Locus of control, 94
Love, 94–96
Lust, 95

Magnetic resonance imaging,
    functional, 34
Medulla, 10
Melatonin, 96–97
Membrane, 97
Meme, 97–98
Memory
    classification of, 99–100
    declarative, 100
    description of, 99–102
    factual, 100–101
    gender differences, 72
    procedural, 100
    short-term, 99
    smell and, 149
    working, 26, 99
Memory network, 98
Meninges, 102–103
Meningitis, 103
Metabolism, 103
Microglia, 74
Midbrain, 1, 8, 103
Mirror neurons, 103–106
Mitochondria, 5, 106
Modularity, 37
Monoamines, 120
Mood, 63
Motor area, 13
Motor cortex, 9, 104–107
Motor degeneration, 49–50
Motor neurons, 105
Movement, 107–110
Music, 110–112
Myelin, 4, 117

Naturalist intelligence, 88
Nature, 112–115
Nerve, 114
Nervous system

central, 39–40, 114–115
circulatory system
    comparison with, 48
definition of, 114
description of, 32, 114–115
peripheral, 114–115, 127–128
Neural intelligence, 89
Neurology, 35
Neurons
    cells that interact with, 116
    characteristics of, 115–117
    definition of, 115
    dendrites of, 116
    description of, 31
    firing patterns of, 36
    granule, 6
    mirror, 103–106
    organization of, 115
    postsynaptic, 133
    presynaptic, 133
    Purkinje, 6
    pyramidal, 6, 41
    reticular formation, 6
    schematic diagram of, 4
    spindle, 150–151
    stellate, 6, 41
    structure of, 115–116
    transmission by, 116–117, 119
    types of, 6
Neuroscience, 35
Neurosis, 118
Neurotransmitters
    acetylcholine, 15
    amino acids, 120
    amino acids and, 16–17
    catecholamines, 38
    classification of, 119–121
    definition of, 118
    description of, 118–119
    dopamine, 31, 57–58
    epinephrine, 15, 66
    histamine, 81
    monoamines, 120
    peptides, 120–121
    release of, 117
    serotonin, 57, 97, 144–145
    types of, 118–119